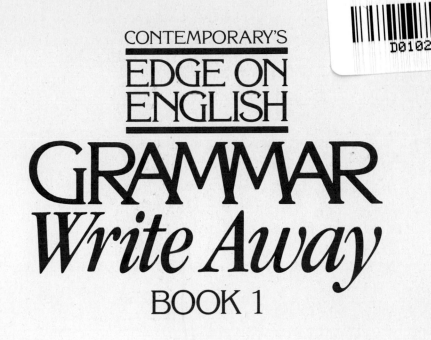

CONTEMPORARY'S
EDGE ON
ENGLISH
GRAMMAR
Write Away
BOOK 1

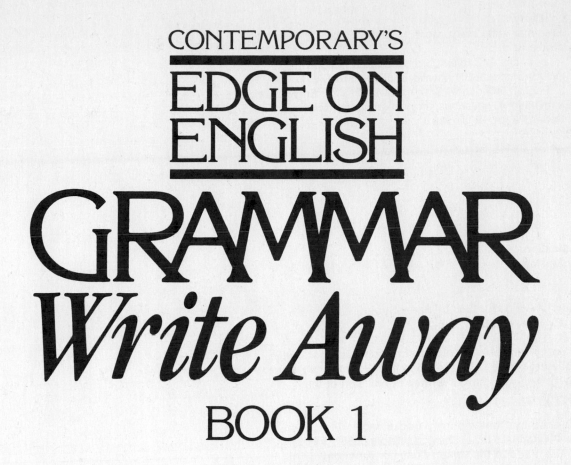

CONTEMPORARY'S

EDGE ON ENGLISH

GRAMMAR
Write Away

BOOK 1

BETSY RUBIN

Project Editor
Patricia Reid

CONTEMPORARY
BOOKS

CHICAGO

Library of Congress Cataloging-in-Publication Data

Rubin, Betsy.
   Grammar write away : book 1 / Betsy Rubin : project editor,
Patricia Reid.
      p.   cm.—(Contemporary's edge on English)
   Includes index.ISBN (invalid) 0-8092-4807-4 (v. 1)
    1. English language—Grammar—1950-   2. English language—
Examinations, questions, etc.   I. Reid, Patricia.   II. Title.
III. Series.PE1112.R78 1988   88-39766
428.2—dc19   CIP

Dedication
For Matthew

Published by Contemporary Books, Inc.
Two Prudential Plaza, Chicago, Illinois 60601-6790
Manufactured in the United States of America
International Standard Book Number: 0-8092-4807-7

Published simultaneously in Canada by
Fitzhenry & Whiteside
195 Allstate Parkway
Markham, Ontario L3R 4T8
Canada

Editorial Director Caren Van Slyke	*Cover Design* Lois Koehler
Editorial Karin Evans Kathy Osmus Sarah Schmidt Lori Lewis-Chapman Deborah Donberg	*Illustrator* Maxine Shore *Art & Production* Princess Louise El Jan Geist
Editorial/Production Manager Patricia Reid	*Typography* Steven McConnaughay J•B Typesetting Co. St. Charles, Illinois
Production Editor Craig Bolt	
Indexer Sandi Schroeder	

CONTENTS

TO THE INSTRUCTOR   vii

TO THE STUDENT   1

PREVIEW TEST   3

1 SENTENCE BASICS   10
What Is a Sentence?   10
Statements and Questions   12
Verbs   14
Subjects   16
Objects   18
Cumulative Review   20

2 NOUNS AND PRONOUNS   21
Nouns   21
A and *An*   24
Singular and Plural Nouns   25
Irregular Plurals   27
Subject Pronouns   28
Object Pronouns   29

3 VERBS   32
Verb Tenses   32
Simple Present   33
Simple Past   36
The Future   40
Cumulative Review   41
The Verb *Be*: Present   43
The Verb *Be*: Past   45
Present Continuous   46
Past Continuous   49
Cumulative Review   51

4 MORE WORK WITH VERBS   52
Present-Tense Negatives   52
Past and Future Negatives   54
Negatives with *Be*   56
Cumulative Review   58
Avoiding Double Negatives   59
Present-Tense Questions   61
Past-Tense Questions   63
Questions with *Be*   64
Cumulative Review   66

5 NOUN AND PRONOUN FOCUS   67
Noncount Nouns   67
Possessive Nouns   70
Possessive Pronouns   74
Reflexive Pronouns   76
Cumulative Review   78

6 ADJECTIVES AND ADVERBS 79
Adjectives 79
Adverbs 81
Adjective or Adverb? 85
Comparatives 87
Superlatives 90
Cumulative Review 93
Comparing with Adverbs 94
Cumulative Review 96

7 AGREEMENT 97
Review of Subjects and Verbs 97
Basic Agreement 99
Compound Subjects 100
Avoiding Double Subjects 103
Interrupting Phrases 104
Tricky Subjects 107
Here/There 111
Cumulative Review 114

8 WRITING CORRECT AND COMPLETE SENTENCES 115
Avoiding Fragments 115
Using Transition Words 120
Cumulative Review 121
Writing Compound Sentences 122
Because 125
Avoiding Run-ons 127
Review 131
Cumulative Review 132
Compound Verbs 133
Cumulative Review 137
Using Commas 140
Parallel Structure 143
When Not to Use a Comma 145
Cumulative Review 148

9 MAKING SENTENCES WORK TOGETHER 149
Choosing the Right Tense 149
Cumulative Review 153
Pronoun Work 154
Pronoun Agreement 156
Cumulative Review 158

FINAL TEST 159

ANSWER KEY 166

INDEX 181

TO THE INSTRUCTOR

Grammar Write Away Book 1, part of Contemporary's *Edge on English* series, is the first book of a two-volume set dealing with common grammar and writing problems. Both books are designed for use either inside the classroom or for independent study. Students can check most of their own work using the answer key at the back although an instructor or someone else with a good grammar background will need to check students' original writing.

ASSUMPTIONS

This book assumes that grammar instruction is most useful when it is taught in the context of *writing*. That is, in order for students to learn and to use grammatical rules, they need to apply them directly to their own writing of sentences and paragraphs. Fill-in-the-blank exercises, while useful focusing tools, are not ends in themselves; students must have the opportunity to use what they have learned in their own original writing. As well as receiving instruction in the writing of good sentences, students are asked throughout the book to write short paragraphs using what they have practiced.

Another assumption is that grammar is best learned in a *context*. This allows students to see how grammar works in real situations; it also makes grammar instruction more interesting and meaningful. For this reason, *Grammar Write Away* uses real-life themes such as child rearing, teen problems, and work situations in its lessons.

A third assumption is that grammar instruction must be *practical*. Grammatical rules are not learned for their own sakes, but rather for their utility in helping students write good sentences and paragraphs. Thus, this book presents the minimum rules necessary, using simple and clear terminology.

The final assumption of *Grammar Write Away* is that students need to learn standard English grammar for academic and occupational success. Thus, the activities in this book are writing, rather than speaking, activities. The instructor may wish, however, to show applications to speaking in formal situations.

At the same time, the instructor need not tell a student that his or her style of speech is "wrong" or "bad." There are many varieties of spoken English, all of which are both acceptable and valued in informal conversation with family and friends. The instructor can point out merely that a certain style is *appropriate* in some situations and inappropriate in others.

SCOPE

Grammar Write Away Book 1 addresses students who are working with basic grammar and writing issues. Attention is given to the following areas:

- How to use different parts of speech—nouns, pronouns, verbs, adjectives, and adverbs
- How to use the three basic verb tenses—past, present, and future—including the continuous aspect
- How to make verbs agree with subjects
- How to write correct simple and compound sentences
- How to avoid run-ons and fragments
- How to use commas, periods, and capital letters correctly
- How to use verb tenses and pronouns correctly in the context of a paragraph

FORMAT

1. Most lessons begin with a sample sentence that illustrates a principle or a common error.

2. In the "Insight" section, students work through a step-by-step analysis of a particular grammar issue. Sometimes an incorrect sentence is used as an example, and students are asked to find the problem. This analysis leads to a simple, easy-to-follow rule.

3. Next, students complete "Practice" exercises that range from controlled and easy (such as fill in the blank) to freer and more difficult (such as original sentence writing). "Proofread" exercises are designed to encourage students to locate and correct errors embedded in paragraphs or longer passages.

4. Special exercises, called "Show What You Know," are interspersed throughout the book. Most of these are writing assignments on interesting topics and require students to use a variety of principles they have learned. While explicit review lessons are included where necessary, the "Show What You Know" exercise should also be regarded as an important form of cumulative review.

5. A fifty-point diagnostic test is included at the beginning of this book to help the instructor determine where students need particular study. A scope and sequence chart at the end of the diagnostic test correlates questions on the test to sections in this book.

6. A 100-point final test appears at the end in order to determine students' progress. A correlation chart also accompanies this test.

APPROACH

Because many lessons build on previous practice, students should work through the entire book. If a particular lesson is especially easy, it may be done quickly but should not be skipped. In a classroom setting, the instructor should write the lesson's opening example on the blackboard and guide students through its analysis according to the steps of the "Insight" section. Students should then go over this section on their own and begin the exercises. For independent study, students can work through the lessons entirely on their own.

Students can check their own answers in the back of the book. Correct answers are given for controlled exercises, and suggestions are made for some of the exercises in which a number of correct answers may be possible. The instructor should be sure to check students' original writing.

In checking sentences and paragraphs, the instructor needs to focus on the point at hand and on previously taught material only. The instructor should not be overly concerned with errors students have not yet learned how to correct.

It should be noted that this book focuses on grammar skills, not writing skills. While the students are expected to use standard paragraph format, they are not asked to write formal paragraphs or compositions. Substance issues like developing a main point or providing support, while important skills good writers need, are not covered in this book.

In addition to assigning "Show What You Know" and other review exercises, the instructor may wish to present his or her own short, periodic quizzes. As mentioned earlier, a final test appears at the end of the book.

A FINAL WORD

The successful application of rules to improve a student's grammar and writing requires time and effort on the part of both the student and the instructor. This process can be both interesting and enjoyable when viewed as a challenge and as the bridge to better communication.

TO THE STUDENT

Why Is Grammar Important?

Ms. Gresham has put an ad in the paper for a salesclerk in her clothing store. She receives this letter in response:

Dear Ms. Gresham:

I seen your ad for a salesclerk in your store, I would like to apply. My experience it is real extensive I has a sales record in the areas of retail clothing, toys. And jewelry. The enclosed résumé give more information about my background, and work history. I looked forward to hearing from you.

Sincerely,

Jonathan M. Stuart

Ms. Gresham is impressed by Mr. Stuart's work experience, but she is shocked by his grammar. It is hard to read his letter because she can't tell where one idea starts and another ends. In addition, Mr. Stuart has used some words incorrectly.

What does Ms. Gresham do? She decides against Mr. Stuart. He just does not sound capable to her.

Mr. Stuart has a grammar problem. It is standing between him and a good job. Perhaps it is keeping him from getting a better education. It probably doesn't make him feel proud of himself.

Mr. Stuart is not alone. Many people have trouble with their grammar—especially when it comes to writing.

If *you* have a problem with grammar and writing, this book can help you. Find out how.

Practical Lessons

The lessons in this book give basic rules that you can use *right away* to improve your writing. The rules are there to be used—not just learned for their own sake!

1. First, **take the preview test** on pages 3–9 to find the areas where you may need the most practice. Then work through each lesson in the book. If a lesson seems too easy, do it anyway. It may help you with later lessons.

2. Most lessons start with an example. Read it carefully, and **work through the "Insight" questions**. These will help you understand the rule. Next, **study the rule box,** which explains the rule in a few brief words.

1

3. Then **work through *all* the exercises.** The "Practice" exercises will help you write correct words and sentences. The "Proofread" exercises will help you learn to find and correct mistakes in a paragraph or passage. These exercises will help you strengthen your own proofreading skills. That is, they will help you learn to spot errors in your *own* writing when you read it over. The writing activities give you a chance to try out the new rules in your own writing. As you work, check back to the rule box if you need to.

4. After you do each exercise, **read it over carefully.** Many of the worst grammar mistakes are just careless errors!

5. Finally, **check your answers in the answer key** that starts on page 166. If you find mistakes, don't be upset. Just take a minute to figure out *why* you made the mistakes so that you won't make them again.

Every so often, you'll have the chance to do a special exercise—"Show What You Know." In many of these exercises, you'll get a chance to write on an interesting topic. This way, you'll be able to express your ideas and practice grammar skills, too.

Take the final test when you've worked through the book.

A Note About Good Grammar

There are many different kinds of English. Each variety is right for its own time and place. Look at the two sentences below:

> Ain't nothin' like the real thing!
> Nothing is as good as the original.

The first sentence is fun and casual. It might be just the right thing to say to a friend at a party. However, it would be the *wrong* thing to write on an essay test or in a work situation. Only the second sentence would be correct in these situations.

To succeed at school and at work, you will need to write *standard* English, and *Grammar Write Away Book 1* will help you. Now look at what Mr. Stuart would write if he had studied this book:

Dear Ms. Gresham:

I saw your ad for a salesclerk in your store, and I would like to apply. My experience is very extensive. I have a sales record in the areas of retail clothing, toys, and jewelry. The enclosed résumé gives more information about my background and work history. I look forward to hearing from you.

Sincerely,

Jonathan M. Stuart

Now Mr. Stuart is in the running! You can be, too. Good luck in your efforts.

PREVIEW TEST

This test covers the main points you will study in this book. Different people have different strengths and weaknesses in grammar, and this short test will help you evaluate yours. There are fifty questions in all. Don't worry about how long you take to answer them. If you do not know the answer to a question, skip it and move on.

Remember that this test is only to help you determine where you need to study in this book. After you have taken the test, check your answers on page 8. The evaluation chart on page 9 will tell you the chapters in this book that you need to focus on.

For questions 1–40, circle the letter of the correct answer. Be sure to read *all* of the answers before you make your choice.

EXAMPLE: A. I _____ a good student.

    a. am   **b.** was   **c.** were   **(d.)** Both a and b

    B. Mary _____ in a studio apartment.

    a. living   **(b.)** lives   **c.** live   **d.** Both a and b

1. We work in _____ downtown.

    a. office   **b.** a office   **c.** an office   **d.** Both b and c

2. The company hired three new _____ last week.

    a. people   **b.** peoples   **c.** person   **d.** Both a and c

3. My coworkers and _____ prefer the day shift.

    a. my   **b.** mine   **c.** me   **d.** I

4. My boss _____ nervous all the time.

    a. be   **b.** is   **c.** are   **d.** Both a and b

5. My company _____ good benefits.

    a. give   **b.** giving   **c.** gives   **d.** given

6. Richard isn't _____ his work carefully.

    a. doing   **b.** does   **c.** do   **d.** did

7. The guard didn't _____ the burglar.

    a. caught   **b.** catch   **c.** catches   **d.** catching

8. How many hours a day _____?

    a. he work   **b.** he works   **c.** do he work   **d.** does he work

9. At 6:00 last night, I _____ hard.

    a. am working   **b.** was working   **c.** were working   **d.** worked

10. Where _____?

    a. is your boss   **b.** your boss is   **c.** your boss   **d.** your boss at

11. He _____ understand the situation.

    a. don't   **b.** do not   **c.** doesn't   **d.** isn't

12. Last year, I _____ decent wages.

    a. make   **b.** makes   **c.** maked   **d.** made

13. The repairman _____ our typewriters yesterday.

    a. fix   **b.** fixed   **c.** fixes   **d.** fixing

14. _____ a few problems in the factory.

    a. There is   **b.** There are   **c.** It is   **d.** They are

15. _____ smokers in our office.

    a. It ain't no   **b.** It isn't any   **c.** There aren't no   **d.** There aren't any

16. The _____ phone isn't working.

    a. secretary's   **b.** secretarys'   **c.** secretarys   **d.** secretaries

17. The _____ cafeteria is inexpensive.

    a. employee's   **b.** employees'   **c.** employees   **d.** Both a and b

18. The _____ went on strike.

    a. worker's   **b.** workers'   **c.** workers   **d.** Both a and b

19. The union leader spoke _____.

    a. emotional   **b.** emotionally   **c.** real emotional   **d.** real emotionally

20. He was a _____ speaker.

    a. strong   **b.** strongly   **c.** very strongly   **d.** Both b and c

21. The people responded _____.

    a. good   **b.** real good   **c.** well   **d.** real well

22. Our company is _____ in the entire city.

    a. the largest   **b.** the larger   **c.** the most largest   **d.** the most larger

23. Our company is _____ than our rivals.

    a. more productive   **b.** more productiver

    c. the most productive   **d.** the most productiver

24. We are a lot _____ than we were last year.

    a. busy   **b.** more busier   **c.** busier   **d.** busiest

25. We work _____ than before.

    a. more quickly   **b.** more quicklier   **c.** quicklier   **d.** quickly

26. The boss gave good raises to Dwight and _____.

    a. I   **b.** me   **c.** mine   **d.** Both a and b

27. That is not Pete's desk. It is _____.

    a. hers   **b.** her's   **c.** her   **d.** she's

28. I don't know _____ on my shift.

    a. no one   **b.** nobody   **c.** anyone   **d.** Both a and b

29. There _____ excuse for sloppy work.

    a. is no   **b.** isn't any   **c.** isn't no   **d.** Both a and b

30. Everyone _____ a friend at work.

    a. need   **b.** needs   **c.** needing   **d.** Both a and b

31. Two people in the office _____ on sick leave.

    a. are   **b.** were   **c.** is   **d.** Both a and b

32. The manager of the downtown stores _____ every store once a week.

    a. visits   **b.** visit   **c.** visiting   **d.** are visiting

33. The printer and the copying machine always _____ down.

    a. breaks   **b.** break   **c.** breaking   **d.** is breaking

34. My boss and I _____ at the office until 7:00.

    a. was   **b.** were   **c.** am   **d.** Both a and c

35. Up-to-date office equipment _____ routine work easier.

    a. makes   **b.** make   **c.** making   **d.** are making

36. The receptionist welcomes visitors and _____ the phone.

    a. answer   **b.** answers   **c.** answering   **d.** answered

37. The secretary made an appointment and _____ it down.

    a. write   **b.** writes   **c.** writed   **d.** wrote

38. The shipping clerk was counting the orders, recording them, and _____ names to the mailing list.

    a. to add   **b.** add   **c.** adding   d. added

39. The cashier should greet all the customers politely and ring up _____ sales quickly.

    a. their   **b.** her   **c.** your   **d.** its

40. Customers should feel free to go up to a salesman and ask _____ for suggestions.

    a. them   **b.** him   **c.** her   **d.** you

For questions 41–46, read each sentence carefully. Decide which sentence or sentences are correct.

41. Which is correct?

    a. The boss he is late every morning.
    b. The boss is late every morning.
    c. The boss late every morning.
    d. All three are correct.

42. Which is correct?

    a. The boss comes into the room and gives orders.
    b. The boss comes into the room. Then she gives orders.
    c. The boss comes into the room she gives orders.
    d. Both a and b are correct.

43. Which is correct?

    a. For example, to move boxes.
    b. For example, asks us to move boxes.
    c. For example, she asks us to move boxes.
    d. Both a and c are correct.

44. Which is correct?

    a. I lost my ID card so I had to get a new one.
    b. I lost my ID card, so I had to get a new one.
    c. I lost my ID card that's why I had to get a new one.
    d. All three are correct.

45. Which is correct?

    a. My supervisor talks I listen.
    b. My supervisor talks, I listen.
    c. My supervisor talks, and I listen.
    d. All three are correct.

46. Which is correct?

    a. I went to the bank, cashed my paycheck, and spent it.
    b. I went to the bank cashed my paycheck, and spent it.
    c. I went to the bank, cashed my paycheck. And, spent it.
    d. Both b and c are correct.

For questions 47–50, read the paragraph and circle the letter of the correct verb for each blank.

          Last year, I _____ a job at a gas station in my neighborhood. The
owner _____ to pay me the going rate. Unfortunately, he _____ up
to his word. Now I _____ to find a better-paying job.

47. a. take   **b.** took   **c.** taking   **d.** taked

48. a. promise   **b.** promises   **c.** promising   **d.** promised

49. a. don't live   **b.** didn't live   **c.** doesn't live   **d.** do not live

50. a. want   **b.** wants   **c.** wanted   **d.** wanting

Answers start on page 8.

Preview Test Answer Key

1. **c.** an office
2. **a.** people
3. **d.** I
4. **b.** is
5. **c.** gives
6. **a.** doing
7. **b.** catch
8. **d.** does he work
9. **b.** was working
10. **a.** is your boss
11. **c.** doesn't
12. **d.** made
13. **b.** fixed
14. **b.** There are
15. **d.** There aren't any
16. **a.** secretary's
17. **b.** employees'
18. **c.** workers
19. **b.** emotionally
20. **a.** strong
21. **c.** well
22. **a.** the largest
23. **a.** more productive
24. **c.** busier
25. **a.** more quickly
26. **b.** me
27. **a.** hers
28. **c.** anyone

29. **d.** is no
    isn't any
30. **b.** needs
31. **d.** are
    were
32. **a.** visits
33. **b.** break
34. **b.** were
35. **a.** makes
36. **b.** answers
37. **d.** wrote
38. **c.** adding
39. **a.** their
40. **b.** him
41. **b.** The boss is late every morning.
42. **d.** The boss comes into the room and gives orders.
    The boss comes into the room. Then she gives orders.
43. **c.** For example, she asks us to move boxes.
44. **b.** I lost my ID card, so I had to get a new one.
45. **c.** My supervisor talks, and I listen.
46. **a.** I went to the bank, cashed my paycheck, and spent it.
47. **b.** took
48. **d.** promised
49. **b.** didn't live
50. **a.** want

Preview Test Evaluation Charts

Use the charts below to determine the grammar skills in which you need to do the most work. Circle any items that you got correct, and pay particular attention to areas where you missed half or more of the questions.

For your convenience, we have provided two charts. This way, you can focus on the areas where you may need the most work. The first chart is for items 1–40 and 47–50. It is keyed by content area. Each item tests only one skill. Because items 41–46 test more than one skill, we have provided a separate chart so that you can see which skills each item tests.

EVALUATION CHART FOR ITEMS 1–40, 47–50			
Content Area	**Item Number**	**Review Pages**	**Number Correct**
Chapter 2			
Nouns	1, 2	21–27	_____ /2
Pronouns	3, 26	28–31	_____ /2
Chapter 3			
Verb Tenses	4, 5, 9, 12, 13	32–50	_____ /5
Chapter 4			
Negatives	6, 7, 11, 15, 28, 29	52–60	_____ /6
Questions	8, 10	61–65	_____ /2
Chapter 5			
Possessives and Apostrophes	16, 17, 18, 27	70–75	_____ /4

Chapter 6 Adjectives and Adverbs	19, 20, 21	79–86	_____/3
Comparative/ Superlative	22, 23, 24, 25	87–95	_____/4
Chapter 7 Subject-Verb Agreement	14, 30, 31, 32, 33, 34, 35	97–113	_____/7
Chapter 8 Compound Verbs	36, 37, 38	133–36	_____/3
Chapter 9 Tense Choice	47, 48, 49, 50	149–52	_____/4
Pronoun Agreement	39, 40	154–57	_____/2
Total for Items 1–40, 47–50			_____/44

EVALUATION CHART FOR ITEMS 41–46

Item Number	Study Pages	Number Correct
41	Double Subjects p. 103 Fragments pp. 115–19	_____/1
42	Compound Verbs pp. 133–36 Run-ons pp. 127–30	_____/1
43	Fragments pp. 115–19	_____/1
44	Compound Sentences pp. 122–24 Run-ons pp. 127–30	_____/1
45	Run-ons pp. 127–30	_____/1
46	Comma Usage pp. 140–42 Fragments pp. 115–19	_____/1
Total for Items 41–46		_____/6

Total Correct on Preview Test
(add scores from both boxes)   _____/50

CHAPTER 1
SENTENCE BASICS

- To recognize complete sentences
- To distinguish between two types of sentences—statements and questions
- To recognize important parts of a sentence—verbs, subjects, and objects

WHAT IS A SENTENCE?

Understanding the Message

You come home from school and find this message from your sister:

○	Called.
	Won the lottery.
	Mitch.
○	

INSIGHT

What does this note mean? *Who* called? Was it Mitch or someone else? And more importantly, *who* won the lottery? Did *you*? Finally, *what about* Mitch? Are you supposed to call him back?

Now you don't know how to feel. Maybe you're a millionaire now, but maybe someone else is. To understand this strange note, you have to go and ask your sister what she meant. This is what she tells you:

"Mitch called. His wife won the lottery. Mitch will call you back later."

You understand the message now because your sister has used sentences in her explanation. A *sentence* is a group of words that tells a complete idea.

PRACTICE

Look at each group of words below. Does it tell a complete idea? If so, circle *YES*. If not, circle *NO*. The first two have been done for you.

YES (NO)   **1.** Your boss.

(YES) NO   **2.** Your boss called.

YES   NO   **3.** Won the company contest.

YES   NO   **4.** You won the company contest.

YES   NO   **5.** Can get the prize anytime before Friday.

YES   NO   **6.** You can get the prize now.

YES   NO   **7.** The prize is.

YES   NO   **8.** The prize is a new radio.

Now use the complete sentences to write a message in the space below. Copy each one correctly. The first has been done for you.

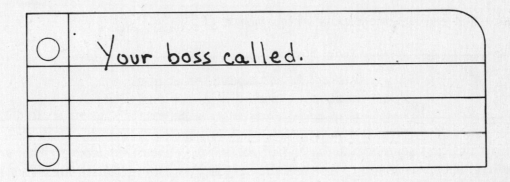

Answers start on page 166.

STATEMENTS AND QUESTIONS

Telling or Asking?

What is she doing?
She is climbing over the wall.

INSIGHT

Both groups of words are sentences, but each group shows a different kind of sentence. The first sentence is *asking* about something. The second sentence is *telling* something. Look more carefully now at the second sentence:

She is climbing over the wall.

This kind of sentence is called a statement. A **statement** is a sentence that tells about something.

A sentence that is a statement ends with a **period** ⬚ .

A statement *tells* about something.
A statement has a period ⬚ at the end of it.

Go back to the first sentence at the top of the page: *What is she doing?* This sentence is not telling about something. Instead, the sentence is asking something. This kind of sentence is called a **question**.

At the end of the question is a mark that looks like this: ? This is called a **question mark**.

A question is a sentence that *asks* something.
A question has a question mark ? at the end of it.

Go back now and look at the first letter of both sentences. What type of letters are they? _____ You're right if you said that both sentences start with *capital letters*.

Every sentence begins with a capital letter.

PRACTICE

Copy each sentence below. (Do not change the order of the words!) If it is a statement, write a period at the end. If it is a question, write a question mark at the end. The first two have been done for you.

1. Helen is climbing over a wall

   Helen is climbing over a wall.

2. What is she doing

   What is she doing?

3. She is taking a test

4. Why is she taking the test

5. She wants to be a firefighter

6. The test is hard

7. Can she pass the test

8. Do you think she will pass the test

9. I think she will pass it

10. She has always wanted to be a firefighter

11. Was someone in her family a firefighter

12. I think her father was one

Answers start on page 166.

VERBS

Action!

Every sentence must have a *verb*. To find out what a verb is, look at the **boldface** words in each sentence below:

> Alice **works** hard at her new job. She **looked** for weeks before she finally **found** it. In her job, she **meets** with many people. She also **writes** reports. She **finished** two reports before she **went** home yesterday.

INSIGHT

Now underline all the **boldface** words in the passage above. Each is a verb that describes an *action*.

An action verb is a word that tells what the action is.

PRACTICE 1

Underline every verb in the paragraph. The first one has been done for you. There are six verbs in all.

> Shawn works hard at his new job in the restaurant. He applied for
>
> many other jobs before he got this one. At work, he cooks a lot of ham-
>
> burgers. He usually makes over two hundred hamburgers every day before
>
> he leaves the restaurant.

Answers start on page 166.

Being Verbs

Most verbs show the action in a sentence, but not all of them do exactly that. Look at the **boldface** words below.

> Alice **is** an office worker now, but before that she **was** a factory worker. Alice and her family **are** very happy about her new job. I **am** happy for her, too.

The boldface words do not describe actions. Instead, they tell what something or someone *is*. They are called *being verbs*. Being verbs can come in many forms, such as *am, is, are, was,* and *were*.

There are two kinds of verbs: *action* verbs and *being* verbs.
***Being* verbs tell what something or someone is or was.**

PRACTICE 2

Underline every action verb and every being verb. There are four verbs in all.

Shawn is a chef in a restaurant now, but before that he worked in a car wash. He earns more money now, so he and his family are happy.

Answers start on page 166.

Forms of Verbs

Sometimes a verb has more than one part. Look at the **boldface** words in this paragraph:

Shawn **makes** good sandwiches. Right now, he **is making** a fish sandwich. This afternoon, he **will make** over fifty of them.

Now underline all the **boldface** words. Notice that sometimes verbs have just one part (*makes*), but sometimes they have more than one part (*is making, will make*).

> **Verbs can be made of more than one word.**

The *base form* of a verb is the starting point for all the forms a verb can take. It is the shortest, simplest form of the verb. For example, *makes, is making,* and *will make* all come from the base *make*. Try an example yourself. What is the base form for *stops, stopped,* and *is stopping*? _____ You're right if you said *stop*.

> **The base form is the shortest, simplest form of the verb.**

PRACTICE 3

Write the base form of each set of verbs below. The first one has been done for you.

1. stops, stopped, is stopping ___**stop**___
2. reads, will read, are reading _____
3. am playing, have played, will play _____
4. is drinking, drinks, will drink _____
5. listened, am listening, listens _____
6. Now take thirty seconds and write down as many verbs as you can think of. Write only the *base forms*. _____

_____

Answers start on page 166.

SUBJECTS

The Alien Jumped Out

Every sentence must have an action. There also must be someone or something *doing* that action: a *subject*. To find out what a subject is, look at the **boldface** words in the passage below.

> **Parker and Johnson** quickly entered the room. The **computer** was beeping. The **lights** were flashing. Suddenly, the **alien** jumped out. Without fear, **Parker** killed it with his laser gun.

INSIGHT

Now answer these questions. The first has been done for you.

Who entered the room? __Parker and Johnson__

What was beeping? _____

What things were flashing? _____

What jumped out? _____

Who killed the alien? _____

You answered each question by writing the *subject* of each sentence. The subject tells *who* or *what* is doing the action. Remember that the verb is the action, so the subject is the person or thing that is doing the action of the verb.

Now go back to the passage and find all the verbs. The first verb is *entered*. What are the rest? _____

You're right if you wrote *was beeping, were flashing, jumped,* and *killed.*

A subject is the person or thing that is doing the action of the sentence.

PRACTICE 1

In the passage below, find the subject and the verb in each sentence. <u>Underline</u> each verb and write *V* over it. Then underline each subject and write *S* over it. The first sentence has been done for you.

        S   V

The <u>alien</u> <u>was</u> dead. Parker called the other crew members. First Collins

arrived on the scene. Then Davis ran into the room. She carefully studied

the dead alien. Parker helped Davis. Collins was too scared to do anything.

Later, Parker and Johnson opened the spaceship door. The alien silently

fell out into space. At last, the spaceship was safe again.

Answers start on page 166.

Finding Subjects and Verbs in Questions

Every sentence must have a subject and a verb. This is true for questions as well as for statements. Look at these two questions:

    Where did the alien live?
    Where is the alien now?

What is the verb in the first question? _____ What is the verb in the second question? _____ You're right if you said *did live* (an action verb with two parts) and *is* (a being verb). What is the subject of each question? _____ You're right again if you said *alien*. The *alien* is what *did live* or *is* somewhere. Now go back and mark *S* and *V* over the subject and verb in each question.

Notice that in a question the subject often is not before the verb. Also, notice that the verb in a question often has two parts that are separated, as in this example:

    Where **did** the alien **live**?

PRACTICE 2

Underline each subject and verb (or verbs) and write *S* or *V* above it. The first one has been done for you.

  V   **S   V**

1. <u>Did</u> the <u>alien</u> <u>live</u> on another planet?
2. What did the alien eat?
3. How did it enter the spaceship?
4. Is it here now?
5. Did Parker kill it?
6. Where are the other aliens?
7. What was Johnson doing?
8. What did Davis discover about the alien?
9. How did Collins get a job on a spaceship?

Answers start on page 166.

OBJECTS

The Object of Her Affection

Every sentence must have a subject and a verb. Many sentences also have another part called an *object*. Take a look at the sentence below.

Amy kissed Allen.

INSIGHT

What is the verb in this sentence? _____ What is the subject? (In other words, *who* did the kissing?) _____ Write *S* over the subject (*Amy*) and *V* over the verb (*kissed*). Who *received* the kiss? _____ In this sentence, *Allen* is the **object** because he received the kiss. Write *O* over the object of the sentence (*Allen*).

> **The object is the person or thing that receives the action of the verb.**

PRACTICE 1

Circle the object of each sentence. Always ask yourself, "Who or what is receiving the action of the verb?" The first one has been done for you.

1. Amy kissed 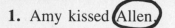 Allen.
2. Amy smiled at Allen warmly.
3. Amy chased the cat all over the house.
4. Amy fed the cat well.
5. Amy called her sister on the phone.
6. Amy loves her brothers.
7. Amy started a project at the office.
8. Amy finished the job quickly.

Answers start on page 166.

Finding the Object

You may have noticed in the practice that each statement had the same subject: *Amy*. However, the sentences have different verbs (*kissed, smiled, looked,* etc.) and different objects (*Allen, the cat, her sister,* etc.).

In each statement, the subject comes before the verb, and the object comes _____ the verb. You're right if you said the object comes after. Sometimes the object comes after a short word such as *at, for,* or *to*. These short words are called *prepositions,* and they tell about the relationship between the object and the rest of the sentence. The object comes after a preposition in these sentences:

Amy looked **at Allen**.
Amy looked **for Allen.**

Here is a list of common prepositions. Can you think of any others?

at	to	near	of	with
in	from	over	by	without
on	around	under	for	during

Objects come after verbs or after prepositions.

You have learned that every sentence must have a verb and a subject. But does every sentence have an object? No, not always. Look at the two sentences below.

Amy cooks dinner.
Amy cooks well.

In the first sentence, *dinner* is the object. Dinner is the thing that Amy cooks. But in the second sentence there is no object. The word *well* describes the way Amy cooks, but the sentence doesn't tell what *things* she cooks. Some sentences have objects, and some do not.

PRACTICE 2

In the paragraph below, underline the subject and verb of each sentence. Then underline the object if there is one. Write S, V, and O over the correct words. (Not every sentence has an object.) The first sentence has been labeled for you.

       S V   O

Amy likes her fellow workers. She loves computers, too. For this

reason, her job is fun. She writes programs all day. She also supervises

other employees. The employees like Amy. They talk to her frequently.

She is helpful and patient.

Answers start on page 166.

CUMULATIVE REVIEW

Show What You Know

Before you do this special exercise, look over the sentence work you have done on pages 10–19. You should understand these terms:

sentence	subject	period ⬜
statement	verb	question mark ?
question	object	capital letter

PRACTICE 1

Copy the dialogue on a piece of paper. Copy every word correctly. Add a *question mark* at the end of every question. Add a *period* at the end of every statement.

A: My name is Arnold

What is your name

B: I'm Betty

A: It's nice to meet you

What are you studying here

B: I'm taking art classes

It's hard because I have a full-time job

A: Where do you work

B: I work in a video store

Are you working now

A: No, I'm a full-time student

PRACTICE 2

Read the paragraph. For each sentence, underline each subject and each verb. Then look to see if there is an object. If there is, underline it. Write *V* over each verb, *S* over each subject, and *O* over each object. The first sentence has been labeled for you.

        S V   O
Betty has a full-time job. She also studies art. Every day, she draws

pictures. Sometimes she paints, too. Her instructors like her work. They

often display her pictures. Betty is very talented. Is she famous yet? No,

she needs more practice first.

Answers start on page 166.

CHAPTER 2
NOUNS AND PRONOUNS

Goals

- To understand what nouns and pronouns are
- To use *a* and *an* correctly
- To form regular and irregular plural nouns correctly
- To understand when to use subject and object pronouns

NOUNS

People, Places, Things, Ideas

Look around your classroom. Then answer these questions. Circle the words that come to your mind.

1. What kinds of *people* do you see?

instructor   boss   students   men   children   women

2. Where is your classroom? What *places* do you think of?

park   school   river   church   building   farm

3. What *things* do you see?

blackboard   dog   TV   chairs   lights   pizza

4. What *ideas* come to mind when you think of your classroom?

fun   education   homework   rule   war   grammar

INSIGHT

All of the words you have circled are called **nouns**. A noun is a word that stands for a person, a place, a thing, or an idea. A noun can be the subject or object of a sentence.

A noun names a person, place, thing, or idea.

PRACTICE 1

Read the paragraph. Write a noun on each line. Make sure that the paragraph makes sense with the words you write! (Sometimes more than one word is possible.) The first one has been done for you.

Mark Johnson is married and has two children—one __boy__₁

and one _____₂. He and his family live in a small _____₃

on a quiet _____₄. Mr. Johnson works in a _____₅, but he

wants to get a better-paying _____₆. That's why he decided to go

back to _____₇ to learn some new skills. Mr. Johnson studies hard.

He is a good _____₈.

You have just written eight nouns on the lines. Now go back and look for three other nouns in the paragraph. (Do not write names.)

9. _____   10. _____   11. _____

Answers start on page 167.

Proper Nouns

Names are also nouns, but they are a special kind of noun called a *proper noun*. Here are some examples of proper nouns:

Mr. Kowa	United States	Rover
Aunt Bess	Rural Route 7	McMaster Company

The first letter of each word in the proper nouns is a _____. You're right if you said they all began with *capital letters*.

How can you tell the difference between a proper noun and a regular, or ***common***, noun? Remember that proper nouns are somebody's or something's *name*. Look at the two sentences below.

Uncle Randy is a doctor.
Dr. Padgitt needs that blood sample right away.

In the first sentence, *Uncle Randy* is the name of one specific person. *Uncle Randy* is a proper noun. However, there are many doctors around. In the first sentence, *doctor* is a common noun.

In the second sentence, *Dr. Padgitt* is the name of one specific doctor out of all the doctors in the world. Here, *Dr. Padgitt* is a proper noun.

> **A proper noun is the name of a *specific* person, place, or thing.**
> **Each word in a proper noun begins with a capital letter.**

PRACTICE 2

Each sentence below has a proper noun that should be capitalized. Cross out that word or words and write the correct proper noun above it. The first one has been done for you.

1. That road will take you to  ~~yates city.~~

2. Take route 66 right into the center of town.

3. Turn left at the corner by the drugstore and slater's shoes.

4. My aunt and uncle live in a house on lilac avenue.

5. The cat and bowser will probably be fighting when you get there.

6. Uncle Randy will yell to aunt sophie to call the vet.

PRACTICE 3

Each sentence below has a common noun that should *not* be capitalized. Cross out that word or words and write the correct common noun above it. The first one has been done for you.

1. My *mother* ~~Mother~~ wants me to visit Uncle Randy.

2. According to Mom, I don't keep in touch enough with my Relatives.

3. However, my Dentist says I can't go to Georgia next week.

4. Because Dr. Osmus wants to do a root canal right away, I can't travel out of State next week.

5. My sister Margo will help pay the Dental Bill.

6. My Brother will go to Yates City in my place.

Answers start on page 167.

A AND AN

A Life of an Employee

She lives in **a house**. He lives in **an apartment**.

INSIGHT

Look at the words in **boldface**. What kind of words are *house* and *apartment*?
_____ (You're right if you said they are nouns.) Now look at the words *a* and
an. Why is it *a* house but *an* apartment? Look at the box below.

an <u>a</u>partment	a <u>b</u>ook	a <u>h</u>ouse
an <u>e</u>xit	a <u>c</u>ard	a <u>j</u>udge

The first thing you need to know is the five *vowel* letters *a, e, i, o,* and *u*. Vowel sounds
are different from consonant sounds. *Consonants* are *b, c, d, f,* and so on.

Use *an* before (circle one)   **a.** a vowel sound   **b.** a consonant sound

Use *a* before (circle one)   **a.** a vowel sound   **b.** a consonant sound

> **Write *a* before a consonant sound. Write *an* before a vowel sound.**

Watch out for some special problems. Read this sentence:

> I'll meet you in **an hour**.

The letter *h* is a consonant. Why is it *an* hour? Pronounce the word *hour* again. Do you
hear the *h*? No! The word *hour* starts with a vowel *sound*. Try another sentence:

> She joined **a union**.

The letter *u* is a vowel. Why is it *a* union? Pronounce the word *union* again. Say it
slowly. You will hear a *y* sound at the beginning. It sounds like "you-nion." This *y*
sound is a *consonant* sound. That is why *a* is used and not *an*.

PRACTICE

Write *a* or *an* correctly in this paragraph. The first one has been done for you.

Jennifer Johnson is **an** employee of ____ tool factory. She gets three
weeks of vacation ____ year, and she has ____ hour off for lunch every
day. She is ____ active member of ____ union.

Answers start on page 167.

SINGULAR AND PLURAL NOUNS

One Car, Two Cars

Roger has a **car**. Nelly has two **cars**. Ron has three **cars**.

INSIGHT

How many cars does Roger have? _____ How many cars does Nelly have? _____
And Ron? _____ Roger has only one car. The noun *car* is **singular**. Singular means
only one. Nelly and Ron both have more than one car. The noun *cars* is **plural**. Plural
means more than one.

Circle all the plural nouns in this passage:

Ron is very rich. He has three cars, a boat, two houses, two swimming

pools, and a private plane.

Did you circle three words? You should have circled *cars*, *houses*, and *pools*. What letter
comes at the end of each plural noun? _____ You're right if you said *s*.

> **Singular means only one.**
> **Plural means more than one.**
> **Most plural nouns end in *s*.**

PRACTICE 1

Add *s* to make each noun plural. The first one has been done for you.

1. a car—three ___cars___

2. one pool—two _____

3. a day—365 _____

4. an hour—forty-eight _____

5. one boy—four _____

6. an egg—a dozen _____

7. a place—many _____

8. an umbrella—a few _____

Answers start on page 167.

Spelling

Usually all you need to do is add *s* to make a plural noun. There are some exceptions, however.

1. Add *s* to most nouns. (car<u>s</u>, pool<u>s</u>, day<u>s</u>, place<u>s</u>, umbrella<u>s</u>)

2. Add *es* when you hear the "iz" sound at the end of the plural. (dress<u>es</u>, dish<u>es</u>, match<u>es</u>, box<u>es</u>)

3. Change *y* after a consonant to *ies*. (baby—bab<u>ies</u>, lady—lad<u>ies</u>, story— stor<u>ies</u>, fly—fl<u>ies</u>) But if the *y* comes after a vowel, do not change it. Just add an *s* to the end. (tray<u>s</u>, play<u>s</u>, boy<u>s</u>)

See Contemporary's *Edge on English: All Spelled Out Book A* and *Book B* for more spelling help.

PRACTICE 2

Write the correct plural form of each noun. The first one has been done for you.

1. toy __toys__
2. city _____
3. dish _____
4. church _____

5. key _____
6. party _____
7. patch _____
8. brush _____

PRACTICE 3

Write a plural noun in each blank of the paragraph. Make sure the words make sense! (Sometimes there is more than one possibility.) The first one has been done for you.

Nelly is not rich, but she is not poor, either. She drives two __cars__ (1), but her apartment has only three small _____ (2). She loves music and has a collection of 150 cassette _____ (3). She doesn't wear jewelry, but she does have three different _____ (4) she can wear on her wrist to tell the time. Nelly likes to wear blue jeans and t-shirts, but she has two formal _____ (5) to wear to weddings and fancy _____ (6). Nelly has many things. The last time she moved, she had to pack about fifty cardboard _____ (7).

Answers start on page 167.

IRREGULAR PLURALS

Women and Children First

David has only one **child**, but Mark has three **children**.

INSIGHT

How many children does David have? _____ Is the noun *child* singular or plural? _____ How many children does Mark have? _____ Is the noun *children* singular or plural? _____

As you can see, the noun *child* is singular, but *children* is plural. Plural nouns end in *s*, so why isn't there an *s* on *children*? There are a few plural nouns that do not follow the rule. These are called *irregular plural nouns*.

Here is a list of common irregular plural nouns. Copy the plural nouns correctly in the space provided.

Singular	Plural	Copy Plural
child	children	*children*
man	men	_____
woman	women	_____
person	people	_____
foot	feet	_____
tooth	teeth	_____

PROOFREAD

Read this paragraph. Find and correct the mistakes in the plural nouns. Cross out every mistake and write the correct word over it. There are eleven mistakes in all, and the first one has been done for you.

~~Childrens~~ *Children* like to ask question about everything. I know because I have three childrens—two boy and one girl. Here is an example. A few week ago, we were riding the bus. My daughter looked at two womens in front of us. They were laughing at a joke. She said, "Mom, why are those two peoples laughing?" Then my baby boy asked, "Mom, when will I get all my grownup teeths?" Next, my older boy said, "Mom, I saved five dollar. Can I buy some comic book?" It is hard to answer all their question, but I try.

Answers start on page 167.

SUBJECT PRONOUNS

He-Man

Read these sentences:

> The man typed the letters.
> He typed the letters.

INSIGHT

What is the verb in each sentence? _____ What is the subject of the first sentence? _____ What is the subject of the second sentence? _____ You're right if you said the verb for each sentence is *typed* and the subjects are *man* and *he*. Notice that the word *he* stands for *man*.

The word *he* is a pronoun. A pronoun is a word that stands for a noun. In other words, a pronoun can be used instead of a noun.

The pronouns that can be used as subjects of sentences are *I, you, he, she, it, we*, and *they*. Notice that the word *I* is always a capital letter.

A pronoun is a word that stands for a noun.
The pronouns that can be used as subjects of sentences are
I, you, he, she, it, we, **and** *they*.

PRACTICE

Read each situation. Write the correct subject pronoun on the line. The first one has been done for you.

1. The man typed a letter. Then __he__ sent it.

2. The woman is staying home today. Tomorrow _____ will return.

3. The people are having a meeting. Soon _____ will make a decision.

4. The phone is working now. Yesterday _____ was broken.

5. The phone on my desk rang, so _____ answered it.

6. The other workers and I studied the plans all morning. At noon, _____ stopped for lunch.

7. The salesman is very good. Last week, _____ sold more than anyone.

Answers start on page 167.

OBJECT PRONOUNS

Us and Them

Some pronouns are used as subjects, but other pronouns are used as objects. Remember, the object in the sentence is who or what *receives* the action. Look at these sentences:

> The man typed the letters.
> The man typed them.

INSIGHT

The verb in each sentence is *typed* , and the subject is *man*. What is the object of the first sentence? _____ What is the object of the second sentence? _____ You're right if you said the objects were *letters* and *them*. Notice that the pronoun *them* stands for *letters*. *Them* is an object pronoun.

> **The pronouns that can be used as objects are**
> ***me, you, him, her, it, us,* and *them*.**

PRACTICE 1

Write the correct object pronoun on the line. The first one has been done for you.

1. The TV show is funny. I like __*it*__.

2. My daughter is playing. I am watching _____.

3. My son is reading. I am helping _____.

4. The baby is sitting on my lap. She is drooling on _____.

5. Our neighbors are arguing. We can hear _____.

6. Our neighbors are too noisy. They are bothering _____.

Answers start on page 167.

PRACTICE 2

Answer each question. Begin each answer with expressions like:

I love . . .   I don't mind . . .   I like . . .   I can't stand . . .

Use the correct object pronoun in each answer. The first one has been done for you.

1. How do you feel about your classroom? _I don't mind it._

2. How do you feel about tests?

3. How do you feel about your school?

4. How do you feel about your community?

5. How do you feel about your neighbors?

6. How do you feel about the leaders of your community?

7. How do you feel about the president?

Answers will vary.

Subject and Object Pronouns

I like John.
John likes **me.**

The words *I* and *me* both refer to the same person. Why are there two different forms? In the first sentence, the pronoun _____ is the subject, but in the second sentence the pronoun _____ is the object. Don't mix up subjects and objects!

PRACTICE 3

In this paragraph, change every underlined noun (or group of nouns) to a pronoun. Use the subject and object pronouns correctly. The first one has been done for you.

> Pete and Debbie live next door to ~~my family and me~~. *(US)* Pete and Debbie
> spend a lot of time at home. Pete is a gardener. Pete often gives
> my family and me fresh vegetables. In return, my family and I lend Pete
> our lawn mower. Debbie does a lot of work around the house. Debbie is
> good at painting. Debbie helped my family and me when we were painting
> our garage. Then my family and I helped Debbie fix her car. Pete and Debbie
> are good neighbors. My family and I like Pete and Debbie very much.

Answers start on page 168.

Common Problems

Watch out for a common problem. Can you find the mistake in the sentence below?

> My family and me painted the garage.

What is the verb? _____ The verb is *painted*. Take a look at the subject now. (Remember the subject does the action of the sentence.) Can *my family and me* be used as the subject? No! The word *me* is an object pronoun only and cannot be a subject. What subject pronoun can be used? My family and _____. The correct sentence is:

> My family and **I** painted the garage.

Try the next problem.

> Pete helped my family and I.

In this sentence, what is the verb? _____ Now find the subject: _____
Helped is the verb, and *Pete* is the subject. Now look for the object of the sentence.
(In other words, who received the help?) Can *my family and I* be used as the object?
No! The word *I* is a subject pronoun. Which word is the object pronoun? _____. Here
is the correct sentence:

> Pete helped my family and **me**.

If you have trouble using subject and object pronouns correctly after the word *and*, here
is a trick to help you. Cross out the part of the subject or object before *and* and see if
the pronoun sounds right.

> ~~Debbie and~~ me went shopping yesterday.
> ??   Me went shopping yesterday.   ??
> I went shopping yesterday.
> Debbie and **I** went shopping yesterday.

Look at another example:

> Pete repaired storm windows for ~~my husband and~~ I.
> ??   Pete repaired storm windows for I.   ??
> Pete repaired storm windows for me.
> Pete repaired storm windows for my husband and **me**.

PROOFREAD

Find and correct the mistakes in the subject and object pronouns. Cross out every wrong
word and write the correct word above it. There are eight mistakes in all, and the first
one has been done for you.

> I
> My family and ~~me~~ have some good neighbors and some bad ones. I
>
> will tell you about the bad ones. Them are very noisy. They fight all the
>
> time. I hear they every night. Also, the parents don't take care of their
>
> little girl. Her is out on the street until midnight. The little boy usually
>
> stays out with she. The mother doesn't seem to mind. Her and the father
>
> just ignore the children. Sometimes the children come to visit my children
>
> and I. Us try to help them.

Answers start on page 168.

CHAPTER 3
VERBS

Goals

- To learn how to use forms of verbs that tell about the present, the past, and the future
- To learn which forms of verbs go with which subjects
- To learn how to use the continuous to talk about things that are or were ongoing

VERB TENSES

Start the Action

Now that you have learned about nouns and pronouns, you are ready to work with verbs. As you know, verbs tell what the action is. But verbs can do more than that: they can also tell *when* the action takes place.

1. Bonnie **plays** bingo every week.

2. She **played** bingo yesterday.

3. She **will play** bingo next Friday, too.

 INSIGHT

As you know, *play* is the base form of the verb. (Remember, the base form is the shortest, simplest form of the verb.) Now write the verbs that appear in the three sentences above: _____, _____, and _____ _____.

Which sentence is about the present? (circle one)   1   2   3

Which sentence is about the past? (circle one)   1   2   3

Which sentence is about the future? (circle one)   1   2   3

The words *every week, yesterday,* and *next Friday* tell when each sentence takes place, but the verbs themselves also show when the events take place. The *s* ending on *plays* says "present," the *ed* ending on *played* says "past," and the word *will* indicates "future."

The present, past, and future forms of verbs are known as **tenses**. In this section, you will learn how to use different verb tenses correctly.

SIMPLE PRESENT

The Here and Now

Baseball is a great sport. We **play** it every summer. I **play** baseball. You **play** it. My children **play** it. My son **plays**. My daughter **plays**. Who doesn't?

INSIGHT

When the writer says, "I play baseball," is she talking about something happening right this minute or something that happens *in general*? (circle one)
a. right this minute   **b.** in general

You are right if you said *in general*. She may play baseball every day, every week, or every summer, but she probably is not playing baseball right this minute. The verbs in the sentences above are all in the *simple present tense*.

> **Use the simple present tense for actions that happen every day or things that are true in general.**

Notice that the verbs in the passage above are spelled two different ways. Write them both here: _____ and _____. One ends in the letter *s* (*plays*), and the other is the base form (*play*).

The box below shows how the forms of the simple present tense should be used.

Rule	Example
I you we they all plural nouns } + BASE FORM	I play. The grandparents play.
he she it all singular nouns } + BASE FORM + *s*	He play<u>s</u>. The dog play<u>s</u>.

PRACTICE 1

Write the correct simple present form: base form or base + *s*. The first one has been done for you.

1. (*play*) I __play__ baseball.
2. (*play*) My daughter _____ baseball.
3. (*like*) My son _____ baseball, too.
4. (*want*) He _____ to be a baseball player.
5. (*go*) We _____ to the ballpark every week.
6. (*stay*) Frank _____ home to see the game on TV.
7. (*tell*) Ronnie and Clara _____ him he should exercise more.

Answers start on page 168.

Spelling

Use the same rules to add *s* to verbs that you use to add *s* to nouns.

● Add *s* to the end of most words.
● Add *es* where you hear the "iz" sound at the end of the word.
● Change *y* after a consonant to *ies*.
● If the *y* comes after a vowel, just add *s*.

There are three important verbs that are exceptions to these rules: *go—goes, have—has, do—does*.

PRACTICE 2

Write *go, goes, have, has, do*, or *does* in the correct spaces.

1. Every week, we _____ to the ballpark.
2. My daughter _____ there twice a week.
3. She _____ three different baseball caps.
4. I _____ just one cap.
5. My son _____ his homework before the game.
6. My husband and I _____ our housework after the game.

PRACTICE 3

Write the correct verb in the simple present tense. Use the correct form. Look at the rules on page 33 if you aren't sure. Spell the words correctly!

Bill Sperry is a football player. He is an unusually strong man who

_____ (*play*) college football. He _____ (*have*) a lot of
    1   2

fans. The fans _____ (*have*) a special name for him. They
            3

_____ (*call*) him "the Ballerina" because he _____ (*dance*)
whenever he scores a touchdown. After every game, Bill _____
(*go*) home, and he _____ (*watch*) the sports news on TV because
he _____ (*want*) to improve his game.

PRACTICE 4

Look at the picture of a famous athlete coming home after a typical game. Then write
complete sentences to answer these questions. Use the simple present tense.

1. What sport does this athlete play? (Begin with "He plays . . .")

2. What team does he play for?

3. Does he have a wife, or is he single?

4. How many children does he have?

5. What kind of pet does he have?

6. What kind of house does he own?

7. What does he do when he gets home?

Answers start on page 168.

SIMPLE PAST

Lost and Found

Yesterday I **lost** my wallet. I **dropped** it down the garbage chute. Two hundred dollars **slipped** down that chute. Luckily, the janitor **found** it, and he **called** me. I almost **cried** with relief. I **decided** to give him a ten-dollar reward.

INSIGHT

When did this story take place? (circle one)

a. in the future   **b.** in the present   **c.** in the past

Circle the seven **boldface** verbs in the passage above. All of these verbs are in the *simple past tense*. Notice that five of the verbs end in the same two letters: ____ ____. You're right if you wrote *ed*. Most verbs in the past tense end this way; they are called *regular verbs*.

In the past tense, regular verbs end in *ed*.

The same past tense form is used for all subjects: plural and singular nouns, *I*, *you*, *we*, and so on.

PRACTICE 1

Write the correct past tense to each of these regular verbs.

1. (*call*) He _____ me on the phone.

2. (*pick*) I _____ up my wallet.

3. (*show*) He _____ me where he found it.

4. (*count*) I _____ the money.

5. (*hand*) I _____ him ten dollars.

6. (*thank*) We _____ each other.

Answers start on page 168.

Spelling

To spell the regular past tense form, just add *ed* to the base. There are some exceptions to this rule, however.

1. Add *ed* to the base form of most verbs. (call<u>ed</u>, show<u>ed</u>, play<u>ed</u>)

2. Add *d* only to verbs that already end in *e*. (decide—decide<u>d</u>)

3. For short words that end in one vowel and one consonant, double the consonant and add *ed*. (grab—gra<u>bbed</u>)

4. For words that end in *y* after a consonant, change *y* to *i* and add *ed*. (cry—cr<u>ied</u>, reply— repl<u>ied</u>) But if there is a vowel before the *y*, just add *ed*. (obey—obey<u>ed</u>)

Check Contemporary's *Edge on English: All Spelled Out Book A* for more spelling reference.

PRACTICE 2

Write the regular past form of each verb. Spell the words correctly.

1. drop _____

2. bake _____

3. drag _____

4. fry _____

5. stay _____

6. stop _____

7. need _____

8. apply _____

PROOFREAD

The writer of this paragraph forgot to put the verbs in the past tense. Cross out the base form of each verb and write the correct past form above it. There are twelve errors in all, and the first one has been done for you.

Yesterday, Sara ~~drop~~ *dropped* her garbage down the chute. She also drop her wallet. She scream, "Oh no!" The wallet contain $200, and Sara need the money for the whole month. Sara cry for a few minutes, and then she dry her tears. She return to her apartment, and she plan for the next month with no money. The next day, the janitor phone with good news. Sara jump with joy and pick up her wallet.

Answers start on page 168.

Irregular Verbs

Not all verbs have a past tense that ends in *ed*; some are ***irregular verbs***. Two examples of these are in the paragraph at the beginning of this lesson: *lost* and *found*. On page 38 is a list of common irregular verbs. You should know the past forms of most of these verbs by the time you finish this book because these words will come up in your writing over and over again.

Common Irregular Verbs

Base Form	Past Form	Base Form	Past Form
be	was/were	know	knew
become	became	lay (put or place)	laid
begin	began	lead	led
bend	bent	leave	left
bet	bet	lend	lent
bite	bit	lose	lost
blow	blew	make	made
break	broke	mean	meant
bring	brought	meet	met
build	built	pay	paid
burst	burst	put	put
buy	bought	read	read
catch	caught	ride	rode
choose	chose	ring	rang
come	came	run	ran
cost	cost	say	said
cut	cut	see	saw
do	did	sell	sold
draw	drew	send	sent
drink	drank	set	set
drive	drove	shoot	shot
eat	ate	sing	sang
fall	fell	sit	sat
feed	fed	sleep	slept
feel	felt	speak	spoke
fight	fought	spend	spent
find	found	stand	stood
fly	flew	steal	stole
forget	forgot	swear	swore
freeze	froze	swim	swam
get	got	take	took
give	gave	teach	taught
go	went	tear	tore
grow	grew	tell	told
hear	heard	think	thought
hide	hid	throw	threw
hold	held	understand	understood
hurt	hurt	wear	wore
keep	kept	write	wrote

PRACTICE 3

Write the correct irregular verb on each line. Use the correct past form from the list on page 38. Use each verb only once.

1. After school, my friend and I _____ home.

2. We _____ goodbye to the other students.

3. We _____ the bus because I was too tired to walk.

4. I _____ a bus coming, so we ran to catch it.

5. My friend _____ his wallet somewhere, and he didn't have any money.

6. I _____ him a favor.

7. I _____ the bus fare for him and for myself.

8. We _____ off the bus at 25th Street.

9. Unfortunately, I _____ my umbrella on the bus.

10. I _____ a new umbrella from a street vendor.

PRACTICE 4

Use your imagination and the words below to write complete sentences about what happened to John. Be sure to use the correct past forms of these verbs. Check the list of irregular verbs on page 38. The first one has been done for you.

1. take—trip _____John took a short trip._____

2. buy—car

3. drive—New York

4. see—the Statue of Liberty

5. ride—the subway

6. eat—hot dog

7. drink—glass of beer

8. lose—his license

9. go—police station

10. pay—a fine

11. get—new license

12. feel—tired

13. leave—New York

Answers start on page 168.

THE FUTURE

The Will to Succeed

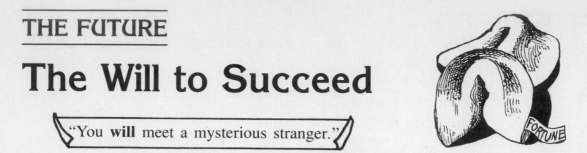

"You **will** meet a mysterious stranger."

"**You'll** succeed in love and work."

Read the fortunes carefully. Each one tells about (circle one)

a. the past   **b.** the present   **c.** the future

In the first sentence, what word do you see in **boldface**? _____ What word comes after *will*? _____ You're right if you wrote *meet*, which is a base verb.

> **To talk about the future,**
> **use the helping verb** *will* **+ the base verb.**

Now go back and look at the second sentence above. Write the first word of that sentence here: _____. *You'll* is a type of word called a ***contraction***; that is, it is two words put together to form one. Here the word *you'll* is really composed of the two words *you will*, with a mark called an apostrophe ⬚ in between.

you (wi)ll   I (wi)ll   he (wi)ll   it (wi)ll
you' ll   I' ll   he' ll   it' ll

Contractions usually show the way people actually talk, but most writers use the complete words in school or business writing.

PRACTICE

Imagine that you have a newborn daughter. You have many hopes for her future. Write about these hopes with the words below. Use *will* in your sentences. You may write either complete forms or contractions. The first one has been done for you.

1. be a happy person   <u>She will be a happy person.</u>

2. be healthy

3. have many friends

4. get a good education

5. find a good job

6. have a wonderful family

Answers start on page 168.

CUMULATIVE REVIEW

Show What You Know

It is time for you to show what you know. Remember what you have studied about complete sentences, the past tense, the present tense, the future tense, and subject and object pronouns. With this knowledge in mind, try writing a short paragraph.

WRITING ASSIGNMENT

What is a paragraph? It is a group of sentences about a common idea. The first sentence of a paragraph usually tells the reader what the main idea of the paragraph is. This sentence is called a *topic sentence*.

Be sure to use the correct form when you write a paragraph. Indent the first sentence—in other words, begin writing a little way in from the margin. Begin each new sentence after the one before it without leaving any extra space. Remember to start each sentence with a capital letter and to end with a period (or question mark if the sentence is a question).

Here is a sample paragraph to help you.

INDENT——→

> Last month, I gave a baby shower for my friends Alice and Ivory and their new baby Kevin. On the day of the shower, I decorated the apartment with streamers and little baby toys. At 2:00 everyone arrived. All the guests loved the baby and wanted to play with him. Alice and Ivory received baby clothes, blankets, toys, and books. Kevin seemed to like his presents. Alice and Ivory were very pleased, and so was I.

Now choose one of these topics, and write a paragraph of about six or seven sentences:

1. **A Celebration**—Think about a celebration you enjoyed. It could be a holiday celebration, a birthday party, an anniversary party, or a baby shower. Before you write, think about these questions. What kind of celebration was it? When and where did it take place? Who came to the celebration? Who brought food or drinks? Who gave gifts? Who received gifts? Did people have a good time? **Use the past tense.**

2. **Your Neighbors**—Think about your neighbors. Write about neighbors you are good friends with or who have been helpful to you. Before you write, think about these questions. What are your neighbors' names (if you know them)? Where do they live? What do they do that you like? How often do you see or talk to them? What do you

help each other with? Do you argue about anything? All in all, what do you like best about them? **Use the present tense.**

After you finish your paragraph, you need to proofread your own work. This is something that all good writers do. This is the time to catch those little mistakes that seem to pop up out of nowhere!

To help you proofread, use this checklist. Read the paragraph over, each time looking for something different.

☑ Every sentence has a *subject* and a *verb*.
☑ The verbs are used correctly.
☑ The words *a* and *an* are used correctly.
☑ The *subject* and *object* pronouns are correct.
☑ Every statement ends in a period.

PROOFREAD

This passage is full of mistakes. Look for mistakes with *a* and *an*, plural nouns, and the present, past, and future tenses. Cross out every mistake and write the correct word over it. There are fourteen mistakes in all, and the first one has been corrected for you.

Ten years ago, Kelly's life was a mess. She ~~have~~ had two childrens, but no job. She was divorced, and her boyfriend treat her badly.

Then her life improve. Why is she happy today? First, she got a education at night school. Then she got a job at a office. She met many new friend at work. She tell her boyfriend good-bye. She became a strong women.

Today, Kelly and her children lives well. Her boy have all kinds of sports trophies. Her girl will starts college in the fall. Also, Kelly met two nice mens at school. Life isn't always easy, but she laugh a lot more than she used to.

Answers start on page 169.

THE VERB *BE*: PRESENT

The State of Being

What is missing from these sentences?

>Marshall his family.
>He a good father.

INSIGHT

You're right if you said that both sentences are missing verbs. Here's one way to fix that problem:

>Marshall **loves** his family.
>He **is** a good father.

The first sentence is fixed with an action verb, the second with a form of the verb *be*. As you may remember, being verbs tell what someone or something *is*. The box below shows some other important present tense forms of the verb whose base form is *be*.

Subject	Verb	Example
I	am	I **am** happy for them.
he she it singular nouns	is	June **is** Marshall's wife.
you we they plural nouns	are	Marshall and June **are** happy together.

As you can see, *be* is an irregular verb. Its past tense will be covered in the next lesson. For now, concentrate on the present tense.

PRACTICE 1

Write the correct present tense form: *am, is,* or *are*.

1. I _____ a student now.

2. The man _____ at home today.

3. She _____ a good mother.

4. They _____ gone for good.

5. We _____ married.

6. That book _____ easy to read.

7. You _____ here at the moment.

8. I _____ always serious.

Answers start on page 169.

PRACTICE 2
Answer each question. Use *am, is*, or *are* correctly.

1. What kind of person are you? (Begin with *I . . . .)*
2. What kind of person is your best friend? (Begin with *He . . .* or *She . . . .)*
3. What kind of people are your neighbors? (Begin with *They . . . .)*
4. What kind of people are you and your classmates (or you and your family)? (Begin with *We . . . .)*

Answers will vary.

Contractions

I am right.
No, **I'm** right!

In the sentences above, the first sentence uses a complete form, and the second uses a _____. You're right if you said the second sentence uses a contraction. Remember that in contractions an apostrophe ☐ takes the place of the missing letter or letters.

I am   he is   she is   it is
I'm   he's   she's   it's

we are   they are   you are
we're   they're   you're

THE VERB *BE*: PAST

Yesterday, When I Was Young

I saw you yesterday. You **were** at Riley's Bar.
No! Yesterday I **was** sick at home all day.

INSIGHT

Are the people talking about now or the past? _____ What word tells you they are talking about the past? _____ You're right if you said that the word *yesterday* tells you it's the past. Now, what are the **boldface** verbs in each sentence? _____ and _____ You're correct if you said *were* and *was*.

> ***Was*** and *were* are the two past tense forms of *be*.

Was	Were
I was	we were
he was	they were
she was	you were
it was	

PRACTICE 1

Write *was* or *were* correctly.

1. Yesterday I _____ sick.

2. You _____ at the bar last night.

3. They _____ loud and rude.

4. We _____ at home all evening.

5. Mark_____ thirsty.

6. The people _____ right here.

Answers start on page 169.

PRACTICE 2

Answer each question. Use *was* or *were* correctly. The first one has been done for you.

1. Where were you at this time yesterday? <u>I was at school.</u>

2. Where were you at 6:00 last night?

3. Where was your best friend at this time yesterday?

4. Where were your neighbors last Saturday night?

5. Where were you and your friends last Saturday night?

6. Think about the last picnic you went to. How was it?

7. How was the weather for the picnic?

8. How were the refreshments?

Answers will vary.

PRESENT CONTINUOUS

What's Happening?

Something strange **is happening**. In the apartment across the way, a woman **is putting** paintings into a big bag. Now she **is taking** the bag outside. A man **is waiting** for her in a car. Now the man and the woman **are driving** away. I **am trying** to decide what to do. Maybe I should call the police!

INSIGHT

Look at the **boldface** verbs in the paragraph above. Each of them tells what is happening *right now*. This form is called the ***present continuous*** because it tells about actions that are continuing in the present (now).

How many parts are in each verb? _____ You're right if you saw that there are two. When a verb has two parts, the first part is called the ***helping verb***. The second part is called the ***main verb***. The main verb always carried the meaning. Notice that the helping verbs in the statement are all forms of *be*.

Now write all the main verbs from the paragraph on the lines below: _____, _____, _____, _____, _____, and _____. In the present continuous, the main verb has an ending made up of the letters __ __ __.

The present continuous tells what is happening right now.
The helping verb is always a form of *be: am, is,* or *are*.
The main verb always has the ending *ing*.

PRACTICE 1

Write the correct present continuous form of the verb in parentheses. One is done for you as an example.

1. (*happen*)   Something *is happening* across the street.
2. (*steal*)   A woman _____ some pictures.
3. (*watch*)   I _____ her.
4. (*wait*)   A man _____ for her in a car.
5. (*go*)   They _____ away.
6. (*wonder*)   My friend and I are nervous. We _____ what to do.

Answers start on page 169.

Spelling

Usually all you need to do is add *ing* to the base verb. There are a few exceptions to this rule, however.

1. Add *ing* to most verbs. (happen<u>ing</u>, steal<u>ing</u>, watch<u>ing</u>)

2. Drop a silent *e* at the end of a verb and add *ing*. (tak<u>e</u>—tak<u>ing</u>, driv<u>e</u>—driv<u>ing</u>). If the *e* is not silent, do not drop it. (agr<u>ee</u>—agr<u>ee</u>ing, s<u>ee</u>—s<u>ee</u>ing)

3. If a short word ends in one vowel and one consonant, double the consonant and add *ing*. (put—pu<u>tt</u>ing, stop—sto<u>pp</u>ing)

See Contemporary's *Edge on English: All Spelled Out Book A* for more spelling reference.

Contractions

Remember that you can make contractions with the verbs *am, is,* and *are*. You can also make contractions when these are helping verbs in the continuous.

> You are working.
> You're working.

PRACTICE 2

Write the correct *ing* form of each verb. Use the spelling rules.

1. put _____
2. take _____
3. pick _____
4. stop _____

5. run _____
6. sleep _____
7. flee _____
8. fly _____

Answers start on page 169.

PRACTICE 3

Picture this scene. You are looking out the window. You can see a young man, an old woman, four children, a dog, two police officers, and a police wagon. Now use your imagination. What is happening? Answer the questions using present continuous.

1. What is the young man doing? (Begin with *He is . . .*)
2. What is the old woman doing?
3. What are the children doing?
4. What is the dog doing?
5. What are the police officers doing?
6. What are *you* doing?

Answers will vary.

Common Problems

Watch out for some common problems. What is missing from this sentence?

He driving away.

How many parts of the verb do you see? _____ You're right if you said one. What type of verb is missing? _____ _____ If you said the helping verb is missing, you're right. Now, which helping verb is the correct one? The correct helping verb is *is*.

He **is** driving away.

What is wrong with the sentence below?

She is takin the pictures.

The helping verb and the main verb are here. How is the ending on the main verb *incorrectly* spelled? __ __ Even though you may not always pronounce the *g*, be sure to always write *ing* when you use the continuous.

She is tak<u>ing</u> the pictures.

PROOFREAD

Find and correct the mistakes in the present continuous. Cross out each mistake and write the correct word over it. If a word is missing, draw an arrow (∧) and write the word above the line. There are thirteen mistakes in all, and the first one has been corrected for you.

            am

I∧looking out my office window. I'm watchin some workers while I

eating my lunch. The workers building a new library for the city. They

workin very hard. One worker is drive a cement truck. Another worker is

operatin a crane. Two more workers drilling holes in the ground. I am

thinkin it would be fun to work with them. My three office friends coming

to the window. They wondering what I looking at.

Answers start on page 169.

PAST CONTINUOUS

What Were *You* Doing?

I **worked** in the garage yesterday.
At 3:15, I **was working** in the garage.

INSIGHT

Look at the **boldface** verbs. Are they talking about now or about the past? _____
In both sentences, the writer is talking about the past.

In the second sentence, the writer is talking about an action that was happening at 3:15.
Was this action finished at that time? (circle one)   **a.** Yes   **b.** No

The second sentence uses the *past continuous* because actions were continuing at a specific time in the past. The work had been going on and was continuing to go on at 3:15 that afternoon.

> **The past continuous tells about an action**
> **that was started and continued in the past.**

Subject	Verb	Example
I he she it singular nouns	was + BASE + *ing*	Lisa **was laughing** for a long time.
we they you plural nouns	were + BASE + *ing*	The ghosts **were scaring** everyone in the house.

What are the two helping verbs? _____ and _____. Notice that both *was* and *were* are past-tense forms of *be*.

PRACTICE 1

Write the correct past continuous form of the verb in parentheses. Use *was* and *were* correctly.

At 3:15 yesterday, I _____ (*work*) in the garage. I _____
_____ (*try*) to fix our car. Sandra and Bobby _____
2   3
(*help*) me. They _____ (*give*) me the tools I needed. But you were
4
too lazy! You _____ (*sit*) on the sofa in front of the TV. You
5
_____ (*drink*) beer. Thanks a lot!
6

Answers start on page 169.

PRACTICE 2

Answer each question using the past continuous. The first one has been done for you.

1. What were you doing at 3:15 yesterday afternoon?

   I was baking cookies.

2. What were you doing at 3:15 yesterday morning?

3. Where were you going when you last drove somewhere in a car?

4. What were you doing the last time the phone rang?

5. What was your best friend doing the last time you went over to his or her home?

6. What were your classmates doing when you walked into the classroom today?

Answers may vary.

CUMULATIVE REVIEW

Show What You Know

In these next exercises, you will draw on what you have learned about verb tenses.

PROOFREAD

Find and correct the mistakes in this passage. Cross out the wrong words and write the correct words above. Draw an arrow to add the missing word. Think about nouns, *a* and *an*, the verb *be*, the continuous, and the future. There are nineteen mistakes in all, and the first two have been done for you.

In 1980, Juan and Nilda Lopez ~~was livin~~ *were living* in Mexico City. Juan was a office worker, and Nilda were a nurse. Them was happy until Juan lost his job. Nilda was workin night and day to support them both. Finally Juan said, "I have a brother and two sister in Texas. Let's go there."

Now they is living in Houston. Juan working in a restaurant. He be unhappy with his job because his pay too low. Nilda is staing home now. They studyin English at a church. They is learning more English every day. They workin hard for the future. They hope they be happy again soon.

Answers start on page 169.

WRITING ASSIGNMENT

Choose topic 1 or topic 2. Write a paragraph of about six sentences on either one.

1. Imagine that you are on a bus, a train, or a plane where there are many strange people. They are wearing strange clothes and doing strange things. Describe the scene. What is each person wearing? What is each person doing? **Use the present continuous** to describe what is happening now. ("I **am riding** a bus. . . .")

2. Try to remember a party that you went to recently or a long time ago. Think about all the people at the party. What were they wearing? What were they doing? What were *you* doing? **Use the past continuous** to describe what was happening ("I **was enjoying** myself at a party last week. . . .")

When you are finished writing, read back over your paragraph.

☑ The continuous is used correctly.
☑ Each verb is right for the subject of the sentence.
☑ Subject and object pronouns are used correctly.

CHAPTER 4
MORE WORK WITH VERBS

Goals

- To use negative forms correctly in all the verb tenses—present, past, and future as well as *be* and continuous
- To write questions correctly in all the tenses

PRESENT-TENSE NEGATIVES

Don't Go Away!

I **love** Gertrude.
I **do not love** you.

INSIGHT

Read the two statements. The second is *negative*; in other words, it is saying "no" to something. Write the **boldface** words in the second sentence here: _____ _____ _____

Here are the rules for forming negatives in the simple present.

Rule		Example
I you we they all plural nouns	+ do not + BASE	I **do not love** you.
he she it all singular nouns	+ does not + BASE	She **does not love** you.

52

Compare the two sentences below:

> I **do not** love you.
> I **don't** love you.

As you know, the second sentence contains a contraction. This contraction is made from the words *do not*. You can also form a contraction using *does not*.

do not   does not
don't   doesn't

PRACTICE 1

Write *don't* or *do not, does not* or *doesn't* in the correct places. Either the complete form or the contraction is OK.

1. Gertrude _____ love you.

2. She _____ like Ron, either.

3. I _____ know a nicer person than Gertrude.

4. We _____ want to be with anyone else.

5. Gertrude's father _____ approve of me.

6. He _____ think I'll be a good husband.

7. Gertrude and her father _____ get along.

PRACTICE 2

Gertrude and her father are arguing about Gertrude's boyfriend. Her father disagrees with her completely and is saying the opposite of everything Gertrude says. Write his statements. Use the correct negative form. The first one has been done for you.

1. Melvin loves me. ___Melvin doesn't love you.___

2. I love Melvin. (Begin with "You . . .")

3. Melvin cares for me.

4. I know him very well.

5. Melvin earns enough money.

6. Melvin works hard.

7. Melvin has a good job.

8. You hate him.

Answers start on page 169.

PAST AND FUTURE NEGATIVES

I Didn't and I Won't!

In this lesson, you will learn how to form negatives correctly in the past and future tenses.

Simple Past

We **bought** a Chevy.
We **did not buy** a BMW.

INSIGHT

Write the verb in the first sentence here: _____. The second sentence is negative. Write the **boldface** words on the lines: _____ _____ _____. The helping verb is _____. The main verb is _____. The main verb uses the _____ form.

> To make the past tense negative,
> use the words *did not* + the base.
> *Did not* can also be formed into a contraction: *didn't*.

Watch out for this common mistake.

> He didn't fixed it.

What is wrong? The helping verb *didn't* is OK. Now look at the main verb: instead of *fixed*, it should be *didn't* _____. Remember that the base form is used with *did not*. Here is the correct sentence:

> He didn't **fix** it.

PRACTICE 1

Read each sentence. Write a negative sentence using the same verb plus the words in parentheses. The first one has been done for you.

1. We bought a Chevy. (*BMW*) __We didn't buy a BMW.__

2. I drove it carefully. (*dangerously*)

3. I parked it in the garage. (*on the street*)

4. Jim and I called our relatives. (*our friends*)

5. We gave Granny a ride. (*Aunt Tilly*)

6. We tried the radio. (*the tape deck*)

7. Jim broke the antenna. (*mirror*)

8. He took it to the dealer. (*a service station*)

Answers start on page 169.

The Future

I **will not** do something foolish.
I **won't** make you sorry either.

INSIGHT

Both these sentences are talking about something that *will not* happen in the future. Write the **boldface** words in the first sentence here: _____ _____. Now write the **boldface** word in the second sentence here: _____.

> **The negative form of the future is *will not* + the base.**
> **The contraction is *won't*.**

PRACTICE 2

Rewrite each sentence to make it negative. Use the complete form for some and the contraction for others. The first one has been done for you.

1. I will do what you say. _I won't do what you say._

2. I will work hard at your gas station.

3. I will work overtime without pay.

4. I will wait until I'm thirty-five to get married.

5. I will eat just beans and rice.

6. I will drink only purified water.

Answers start on page 169.

NEGATIVES WITH *BE*

I'm Not Going to Take It!

I **wasn't** at the bar last night, and I **am not** there now!

INSIGHT

This person is making two *negative* statements. Look at the **boldface** words. Which verb is a contraction? _____ Following is a list of negative contractions using the verb *be*.

is not	are not	was not	were not
isn't	aren't	wasn't	weren't

Note: *Am not* cannot be made into a contraction.

What is wrong with this sentence?

He **ain't** here right now.

The answer is simple: the word *ain't*!

> **Never use *ain't*.**

How can the sentence be fixed? Use the correct present tense form of *be*, in either the complete form or as a contraction.

He **is not** here right now.
He **isn't** here right now.

PRACTICE 1

Write the correct negative forms of *be*. Use the complete form or the contraction. The first one has been done for you.

I am a serious person. I ___am not___ a joker. I _____ a
                             1   2
drinker or a smoker. My brother Lorenzo is the opposite. He _____
                                                              3
at all serious. He and I are completely different. We _____ alike
                                                        4
in any way.

When we were children, we were different, too. I was a good student,

but Lorenzo _____ interested in school. Lorenzo loved basketball

        5

and football, but I _____ good at sports. Our parents didn't mind

                6

our differences. They _____ upset or worried. In fact, they were

                  7

happy with us both.

Answers start on page 170.

The Continuous

I **am not** joking.
You're not listening to me.
He **isn't doing** the right thing.

To write negative sentences in the present continuous, use the negative just as you would
for the forms of *be*, then add the main verb + *ing*. Remember, never use *ain't*.

PRACTICE 2

You and your sister are having an argument about your brother Joe. You say the opposite
of whatever your sister says. Write down what you say. Make your sentences *negative*.
Use either complete forms or contractions. The first one has been done for you.

1. I am listening to you. _You are not listening to me._

2. I am telling the truth. (Begin with *You* . . .)

3. Joe is working very hard.

4. He is treating his family well.

5. They are getting along fine.

6. We are helping them enough.

7. You are meddling in their lives.

Answers start on page 170.

CUMULATIVE REVIEW

Show What You Know

You have studied different verb tenses: the simple present, present continuous, simple past, past continuous, and future. You have also studied the correct negative forms of all these tenses. Take some time now to review all these different forms.

PRACTICE

Write the correct form of a verb on each line. Think about the meaning and the tense. Use a negative where appropriate. Many verbs will have more than one part. The first one has been done for you.

Last year, Harvey **had** an unusual experience. One morning in
1

May at about 6:00, he _____ his car to work. No one else
2

was on the road. Suddenly, he _____ up and _____ a strange
3   4

white object in the sky. It _____ _____ through the air.
5 (neg.)

It was just standing still, and it _____ a humming sound. Harvey
6

_____ on the brakes and _____ out of the car. He _____
7   8   9

to himself, "It's a UFO!" At first, he _____ _____ what to do. Then
10 (neg.)

he picked up his car telephone and _____ the police.
11

This is what he said: "Hello, police? I _____ from my car
12

phone on Fairview Road. I want to report a UFO! I can see it right now.

It _____ _____—it is just hanging in the sky. It _____
13 (neg.)   14

a weird sound. I'm afraid that it _____ _____ here forever, so please
15 (neg.)

come quickly or you _____ it!"
16

Unfortunately, the UFO _____ before the police _____.
17   18

No one else _____ the UFO, so no one believed Harvey's story.
19

Today, Harvey still believes in his UFO, but he _____ _____
20 (neg.)

about it to anyone. Every morning, he just _____ out his car window
21

and hopes that he'll see it again.

Answers start on page 170.

AVOIDING DOUBLE NEGATIVES

Negative Attention

There ain't no sunshine in my heart now that she is gone.

INSIGHT

If this sentence were a line in a popular song, you would probably understand what the singer meant. But is the sentence grammatically correct? _____ You're right if you said no. There are two things wrong here. First, remember the rule you studied before: Never use _____. You're right if you wrote *ain't*. But is the sentence OK if all you do is replace *ain't* with *isn't*?

There **isn't** no sunshine in my heart now that she is gone.

No! The problem is that there are two negative words in the sentence. Write them here: _____ and _____. You're correct if you wrote *isn't* and *no*.

Use just one negative word at a time.

You can fix the sentence in two different ways:

There **isn't any** sunshine . . .   There **is no** sunshine . . .

In the first sentence, there is just one negative word. What is it? _____ In the second sentence, there is just one negative word. What is it? _____ Each sentence is correct because each has just one negative.

Here is a list of common negative words:

no	no one	isn't	don't	won't
not	nobody	aren't	doesn't	can't
never	nothing	wasn't	didn't	
	nowhere	weren't		

Note: The words *any, anyone, anybody, anything, anywhere,* and *ever* are not negative.

PRACTICE 1

Read each sentence and decide if it is correct or incorrect. To help you decide, draw a circle around each negative word. Then write *correct* or *incorrect* in the blank. The first one has been done for you.

incorrect 1. There (isn't)(no) room for mistakes.

_____ 2. We don't have any problems.

_____ 3. She never goes anywhere alone.

_____ 4. They didn't see nothing in the room.

_____ 5. There are no bugs in this house.

_____ 6. Don't you have no brothers and sisters?

_____ 7. Does no one want my advice?

_____ 8. I can't get no satisfaction.

PRACTICE 2

Read each sentence and pick the correct word to write on the line. To help you, circle any negative word you might see in the sentence. The first one has been done for you.

1. We (don't) have **any** time for that. (*any/no*)

2. There _____ nothing in my pockets. (*is/isn't*)

3. I have _____ idea where she is. (*any/no*)

4. I'm not _____ millionaire. (*a/no*)

5. There _____ any good shows on TV tonight. (*are/aren't*).

6. _____ is in the room—it's empty. (*Anyone/No one*)

7. Please don't tell me _____ bad about him. (*anything/nothing*)

8. He doesn't have _____ opinion on that. (*an/no*)

PROOFREAD

Find and correct the errors in this passage. Sometimes there is more than one way to correct a mistake. Cross out the wrong word and write the correct one above it. There are twelve errors in all, and the first one has been corrected for you.

Kathy left Jeff because he never did ~~nothing~~ *anything* nice for her. He didn't buy her no flowers, and he didn't do no housework. In fact, he never did nothing to help her. However, he saw nothing wrong with his behavior.

When Kathy left, Jeff was hungry because there wasn't no food in the house. The house got dirty because no one cleaned it. In time, he learned to shop and to clean, but he still didn't have no one to talk to. He thought, "There ain't no one for me to care about. There wasn't nobody as nice as Kathy. I can't get nowhere in life without her."

So Jeff called up Kathy and told her he never meant her no harm. Kathy gave Jeff another chance, and they're together today. Jeff ain't perfect, but now he does his best.

Answers start on page 170.

PRESENT-TENSE QUESTIONS

Ask Me Anything

Do you **like** jazz?
What kind of music **does** she **like**?

INSIGHT

Each question has two **boldface** words: a helping verb and a main verb. Is the main verb *like* in each question the base form or the base form + *s*? _____ What are the two helping verbs? _____ and _____ You're right if you said the main verb is the *base form* and the helping verbs are *do* and *does*. *Do* or *does* is an important part of most questions in the simple present tense.

Which subjects take *do* and which take *does*? This is similar to the negative forms. Write *do* and *does* on the correct lines.

Use _____ for *I, you, we, they*, and plural nouns.

Use _____ for *he, she, it*, and singular nouns.

Watch out for these common mistakes:

What kind of music you like?
You like jazz?

One important word is missing from each question—the helping verb. Which helping verb do you need here? _____ Here are the correct questions:

What kind of music **do** you like?
Do you like jazz?

PRACTICE 1

Write *do* or *does* and the base verb correctly on the lines. The base verb is in parentheses. The first one has been done for you.

1. (*like*) __Do__ you __like__ jazz?

2. (*like*) What kind of music _____ you _____?

3. (*have*) _____ Rhonda _____ a stereo?

4. (*have*) What kind of stereo _____ she _____?

5. (*keep*) Where _____ she _____ her stereo?

6. (*like*) _____ Rhonda and Jerry _____ to dance?

7. (*give*) How often _____ they _____ parties?

Answers start on page 170.

PRACTICE 2

Make up your own questions with *do* and *does* using this chart. The first two have been done for you.

Question Word	Helping Verb	Subject	Main Verb	Other
Where	do	you	eat	lunch?
░░░░░░	Does	Tonya	like	Larry?
Why		they		
░░░░░░	Do			
What		she		to eat?
		Tony		
Where			work?	

Answers will vary.

PRACTICE 3

Darleatha has a handsome cousin. She wants to introduce him to her best friend, Tonya. Tonya has many questions about Darleatha's cousin. Fill in Tonya's questions in the dialogue below. Use the simple present tense. The first two have been done for you.

DARLEATHA: I want you to meet my cousin Larry. He's coming to visit.

TONYA: 1 Where does he live ?

DARLEATHA: He lives in Houston.

TONYA: 2 Does he have a job ?

DARLEATHA: No, he doesn't have a job. He is a student.

TONYA: Oh, I see. Tell me more about him.

3 _____

DARLEATHA: He likes rock and rhythm and blues.

TONYA: 4 _____

DARLEATHA: He likes adventure and sci-fi movies.

TONYA: 5 _____

DARLEATHA: Yes, he has a few hobbies. He collects beer cans, and he also reads a lot.

TONYA: That's interesting. 6 _____

DARLEATHA: Well, he is very short, but he is really cute.

TONYA: Wow! Now tell me the truth. 7 _____

DARLEATHA: No, he doesn't have a girlfriend. That's why I want him to meet you!

Answers start on page 170.

PAST-TENSE QUESTIONS

Didn't I See You?

A police officer is talking to a young man. You can hear only the officer's voice because the young man is speaking very softly.

> "I want to know your every move on the night of August 7. Did you talk to anyone that night?"

> "Did your friends see you?"

> "Where did you go?"

> "How long did you stay there?"

INSIGHT

The officer asked the man four questions in the past tense. What helping verb did the officer use in each question? _____ Now look at the *main verb*. Is the main verb the base or the past tense form? _____ You're right if you said the helping verb in each question was *did* and the main verb was the base form.

Rule	Example
Did + SUBJECT + BASE	**Did** you **go**? **Did** they **see** you?

PRACTICE

In the chart below, write some more questions the police officer might ask. (Use *did*.)

Question Word(s)	Helping Verb	Subject	Main Verb	Other
/////	Did		talk	
/////				
Where		you		
How long				
			get	home?
/////	Did			
Why				

Answers will vary.

QUESTIONS WITH *BE*

Are You Lonesome Tonight?

Are you at home now?
Yes, of course!
Well, I tried to call you last night. Where were you?
I was at work until eleven.

INSIGHT

There are two questions in the dialogue. Underline them. Which question is about the present? _____ Which question is about the past? _____ You're right if you said the first question is about the present and the second question is about the past. The subject in both questions is _____. You're right if you said that *you* is the subject. In a question with the verb *be*, which is first, the verb or the subject?
_____

In a question with the verb *be*, the verb comes before the subject.

PRACTICE 1

Write the missing form of *be* for each question: *is, are, was,* or *were.*

1. Where _____ you last night?

2. How _____ you today?

3. How _____ your children today?

4. _____ your children at the food fair last Saturday?

5. _____ your wife unhappy with her old job?

6. _____ she happy with the job she has now?

PRACTICE 2

These questions are all mixed up. Put the words in the right order. Write the correct question. The first one has been done for you.

1. you are how? **How are you?** 4. in a fight they were?

2. Bobby at home is?   5. still mad why he is?

3. where he was yesterday?   6. scared were you?

Answers start on page 170.

The Continuous

What are you eating?
Are you eating a taco?

What is the subject of each question? _____ Where does the subject *you* go? It goes _____ the helping verb and the main verb. You're right if you said it goes *between* the helping verb and the main verb. Watch out for this common problem:

What he eating?
He eating a hot dog?

In these two questions, the writer has forgotten the _____ verb. In this case, which helping verb is needed? _____ Here are the correct questions:

What **is** he eating?
Is he eating a hot dog?

Remember to use correct form of the helping verb *be* for the continuous.

PRACTICE 3

You and Dino are at a party. Dino likes a young woman named Lucy. Dino won't wear his glasses, so he is asking you to tell him everything that Lucy is doing. Write Dino's questions on the lines. Use the present continuous correctly. The first one has been done for you.

DINO: Can you see Lucy?
 YOU: Yes. She is here, just standing around.
DINO: 1   **Where is she standing?**
 YOU: She is standing by the food table.

DINO: 2 _____
 YOU: She is eating and drinking.

DINO: 3 _____
 YOU: She is eating chips and dip.

DINO: 4 _____
 YOU: She is wearing a red dress and cowboy boots. Wait! She is walking away from the table.

DINO: 5 _____
 YOU: She is going to the door. No. She is turning around. She is coming over here!

DINO: 6 _____
 YOU: Why? Because she wants to meet you, you chump!

Answers start on page 171.

CUMULATIVE REVIEW

Show What You Know

What you doing? What you want?

Something is missing from these questions. By now you should know that the questions need helping verbs to make them grammatically correct.

What **are** you doing? What **do** you want?

Helping Verb	Main Verb	Example
Present: *am, is,* or *are*	BASE + *ing*	**Is** he **singing**?
Past: *was* or *were*	BASE + *ing*	**Were** you **laughing**?
Present: *do, does*	BASE	**Does** he **smile**?
Past: *did*	BASE	**Did** the bottle **break**?
Future: *Will*	BASE	**Will** he **call** you?

PRACTICE 1

Write the correct helping verb and the correct form of the main verb (base or *ing* form). The first two have been done for you.

1. (*like*) **Do** they **like** to hunt?
2. (*hunt*) **Are** they **hunting** right now?
3. (*sleep*) _____ the children _____ now?
4. (*sleep*) _____ they _____ eight hours every night?
5. (*do*) What _____ Mary _____ after school every day?
6. (*read*) _____ you _____ when I came home last night?

Answers start on page 171.

PRACTICE 2

Imagine that you have a teenage son or daughter. Your child comes home very late, and you are angry and concerned. What questions would you ask your child? Write down five questions you would want to ask him or her. Use past, present, and future.

Answers will vary.

CHAPTER 5
NOUN AND PRONOUN
FOCUS

---Goals---

- To distinguish between count and noncount nouns
- To use apostrophes correctly with singular, plural, and irregular possessive nouns
- To use possessive and reflexive pronouns correctly

NONCOUNT NOUNS

Water, Water Everywhere

The water is in five cups.

INSIGHT

Get a few glasses or cups. Fill one up with water. Can you count the cups? Sure! You may have two, three, four cups or more. The word *cup* is a **count noun**.

Now start playing around with the water. Pour a little into one cup, a lot into another cup, just a drop into another . . . Then stop and look at what you've got. You can count the drops, but can you count the water? Can you say "one water," "three waters," "five waters"? No way! *Water* is a **noncount noun**.

> **If you can't count it, it's a noncount noun.**

Noncount nouns use the same verb forms as singular nouns. Look at these examples:

NONCOUNT: The water **is** on the floor.
SINGULAR: The cup **is** on the floor.
PLURAL: The dishes **are** on the floor.

PRACTICE 1

Here is a list of nouns. Write *count* or *noncount* in each blank.

_____ 1. cup   _____ 7. health

_____ 2. water   _____ 8. wallet

_____ 3. banana   _____ 9. luggage

_____ 4. air   _____ 10. honesty

_____ 5. gasoline   _____ 11. fight

_____ 6. wheel   _____ 12. milk

PRACTICE 2

Write the correct present tense of each verb to complete the sentence. The subjects may be singular, plural, or noncount.

1. Your shoes _____ shiny. (*look*)

2. Your hair _____ nice. (*look*)

3. Your cologne _____ good. (*smell*)

4. Your hands _____ warm. (*feel*)

5. Your voice _____ husky. (*sound*)

6. Your teeth _____ sharp. (*look*)

7. Your kindness _____ comforting. (*be*)

8. Your temper _____ worse every year, though. (*get*)

Answers start on page 171.

Quantity Expressions

a lot of butter—a lot of bananas
some butter—some bananas
any butter—any bananas
a little butter—a few bananas
not much butter—not many bananas
a large amount of butter—a large number of bananas

Look at the words above. Is the word *butter* a count or noncount noun? _____
What about *bananas*? _____ *Butter* is a noncount noun (you can't have *many butters*) while *bananas* is a plural count noun (you can have *many bananas*).

Now look at the expressions. Both plural count and noncount nouns can go with the expressions _____, _____, and _____. Only noncount nouns can go with the expressions _____, _____, and _____. Only plural count nouns can go with the expressions _____, _____, and _____.

Either Noncount or Plural	Only Noncount	Only Plural
a lot of	a little	a few
some	much	many
any	an amount of	a number of
more	less	fewer
most		

PRACTICE 3

Choose the correct word and write it on the line.

1. (*few/little*) I bought a _____ oranges at the store.
2. (*many/much*) How _____ rooms do you have in your apartment?
3. (*many/much*) How _____ luggage did you bring?
4. (*few/little*) Can you lend me a _____ dollars?
5. (*few/little*) I need a _____ advice.

Answers start on page 171.

PRACTICE 4

Now you decide on a noun for each line. Choose either a *plural count noun* or a *noncount noun*. Sometimes either type is possible. The first one has been done for you.

1. I don't have any __luck__. (or: I don't have any __problems__.)
2. We have a few _____.
3. Do you know some _____?
4. Can you pour me a little _____?
5. I found a number of _____ in the closet.
6. I need more _____.
7. How many _____ will you buy?
8. How much _____ did you borrow?
9. I don't want any _____ from him!

Answers will vary.

POSSESSIVE NOUNS

Franco's Wages

Many people are not sure when to use apostrophes ☐ in their writing. You have already learned how to use them in contractions. In this lesson you will learn how to use apostrophes in *possessive nouns*—nouns that show that somebody owns something. Here are some examples: *Franco's wages, the workers' paychecks, the people's health.*

Singular Nouns

Whose money is this?
I think it belongs to LaTisha. It must be **LaTisha's** money.

INSIGHT

Copy the **boldface** word here: _____ This word really has two parts: the name *LaTisha* and the ending _____. (Remember that ☐ is called an *apostrophe*.) The *'s* ending means that the money *belongs to* LaTisha. LaTisha is the owner. The *'s* ending is called a *possessive* form—it says that someone possesses, or owns, something. The owner can sometimes be a thing, not a person, as in this example: *The job's pay is too low.*

Now, are the words *LaTisha* and *job* singular or plural? _____ You're right if you saw that *'s* is added to singular nouns.

> **Add *'s* to singular nouns.**
> **The *'s* ending means that something or someone is the owner.**

PRACTICE 1

Rewrite each sentence, adding the possessive *'s* ending to the word in parentheses (   ). Do not copy the parentheses. The first one has been done for you.

1. This is (*someone*) money. <u>**This is someone's money.**</u>
2. I think it is (*LaTisha*) money.
3. (*Franco*) wages are very good.
4. The (*company*) pay scales are high.
5. His (*wife*) salary is too low.
6. Her (*supervisor*) wages are too low.
7. The (*family*) income is all right.

Answers start on page 171.

PRACTICE 2

Think of five people you know. They could be your instructor and four classmates, or five friends or family members. Then write a sentence about the belongings of each person. Tell what is special about the belongings. Write *five* sentences—one for each person.

EXAMPLE: The instructor's papers are in a folder.
Paul's notebook is under the chair.
Dolores's jacket has big pockets.

Answers will vary.

Plural Nouns

LaTisha and Franco Brown have two daughters.
The **Browns'** daughters are good in school.
The **girls'** grades are high.

INSIGHT

Are the **boldface** words singular or plural? _____ What tells you that these plural nouns are possessives? _____ You're right if you said ⸂ (an apostrophe).

> **To make a plural noun that ends in *s* possessive,**
> **add an apostrophe ⸂ after the *s*.**

PRACTICE 3

Rewrite each sentence, adding an apostrophe ⸂ to the end of each plural name or noun in parentheses. Watch out—some sentences have two possessives.

1. The (*Browns*) two daughters are smart.

2. The (*girls*) math homework is better than the other (*students*) work.

3. The (*Browns*) two sons are also bright.

4. The (*boys*) reading work is better than their (*classmates*) work.

5. Their math and reading (*teachers*) reports are always good.

Answers start on page 171.

Irregular Plural Possessives

Look at the next sentences.

The **children's** grades are excellent.

Is the word *children* singular or plural? _____ You're right if you said plural. But does the word *children* end in *s*? No. This word is an irregular plural. (Look back to page 27.) Irregular plurals like *children, men, women,* and *people* are treated the same as singular nouns—add *'s* to make the possessive.

Add *'s* to irregular plural nouns that do not end in *s*.

PRACTICE 4

Rewrite the paragraph, adding the possessive *'s* to each irregular plural in parentheses.

_____ (*People*) salaries are not always fair. Sometimes
1
_____ (*men*) wages are higher than _____ (*women*) wages
2   3
for the same type of job. Often _____ (*women*) incomes alone are
4
not enough to cover their _____ (*children*) needs.
5

Answers start on page 171.

Common Problems

Remember that *'s* or ☐ at the end of nouns is a sign of the possessive. That is, it tells us that someone or something is the owner. Keeping this in mind, try to see what is wrong with this sentence:

The students' are all here.

First ask yourself: Is this sentence talking about something that belongs to someone? _____ You're right if you said *no*. It is not possessive, so the apostrophe does not fit here. The writer simply means this:

The **students** are all here.

The word *students* is a plural noun. A simple plural noun needs just an *s* ending and not an apostrophe. Try another problem:

Some baby's cry all night.

Again, ask yourself some questions. Is this sentence talking about something that belongs to a baby? _____ Or is it talking about more than one baby? _____ What is the correct way to spell the plural of the word *baby*? _____ The complete correct sentence is this:

Some **babies** cry all night.

PROOFREAD

Look for the mistakes in possessive forms and plural forms. Cross out every error and write the correct word above it. There are six mistakes in all, and the first one has been corrected for you.

                              adults

Sometimes it is hard for ~~adults'~~ to be in school. This is because adults

are often parent's and worker's as well as student's. An adults life can be

too full of worry's about home and work.

Answers start on page 171.

Summary

Let's put together all you have learned about plural and possessive nouns.

Type of Word	What to Do	Example
plural noun	add *s*	The **books** are on the shelves.
singular possessive	add *'s*	The **car's** brakes need grease.
irregular plural possessive not ending in *s*	add *'s*	The **women's** room is out of order.
plural possessive ending in *s*	add '	Five **cars'** engines were no good.

PROOFREAD

Cross out the incorrect possessives and write the correct words above. There are eight mistakes in all, and the first one has been done for you.

                    Chang's

Martin ~~Chang~~ job is a good one. Mr. Changs salary is $20,000. Mr.

Chang has three female helpers'. The helper's wages are much lower. Mr.

Chang's wife has a lot to say about this. She thinks the womens' pay is

too low. Mr. Chang disagrees with his wifes opinion. He thinks people's

salary's depend on their jobs. He thinks his assistants pay is fair.

Answers start on page 171.

POSSESSIVE PRONOUNS

Yours, Mine, and Ours

This is Jim's dog.
This is **his** dog.

INSIGHT

The first sentence above talks about Jim's dog. In the second sentence, which word stands for *Jim's*? _____ You're right if you wrote *his*. The word *his* is a *possessive pronoun*, a pronoun that is used like a possessive noun to show ownership.

Pronoun	Example
my	These are **my** boots.
your	**Your** coat was in the hall closet.
his	He looked for **his** cat.
her	This is **her** dog.
its	The dog buried **its** bone.
our	**Our** house is near a marsh.
their	**Their** car never starts.

Notice that these pronouns are always used before a noun. In other words, with these possessives, the thing that is owned is always mentioned (*my boots*). Notice also that apostrophes are *not* used. What is wrong with this sentence?

The hamster is running in it's wheel.

As you learned on page 144, *it's* spelled with an apostrophe is a contraction for *it is*. If you aren't sure whether to use an apostrophe or not, try substituting the words *it is*:

The hamster is running in **it is** wheel.

Does this sentence make sense? No! *Its* must be a possessive pronoun in this sentence; that is, the wheel belongs to the hamster. *Its* as a possessive pronoun is not spelled with an apostrophe.

The hamster is running in **its** wheel.

PRACTICE 1

Read each sentence given, then write a sentence using the correct possessive pronoun with the correct noun. Use your imagination for the rest of the sentence you write. The first one has been done for you.

1. Chris and I have a car. <u>Our car is ten years old.</u>

2. I have a TV.

3. The TV has an antenna.   6. You have a stereo.

4. Mr. Turner has a job.   7. We have a house.

5. Mrs. Turner has a job.

Answers will vary.

Another Type of Possessive Pronoun

This dog is Janet's.
This dog is **hers**.

INSIGHT

In the first sentence, the word *Janet's* comes at the end. In the second sentence, which word stands for *Janet's*? _____ You're right if you wrote that *hers* stands for *Janet's*. There is no noun right after the possessive pronoun *hers*. In other words, the thing that is owned is not mentioned right after the possessive. If the owned thing is *not* right after the possessive, use the type of possessive pronoun shown below.

Pronoun	Example
mine	These boots are **mine**.
yours	The coat in the hall closet is **yours**.
his	The cat that's missing is **his**.
hers	This dog is **hers**.
its	The bone is **its**.
ours	The house near the marsh is **ours**.
theirs	The car that never starts is **theirs**.
Do not use an apostrophe with possessive pronouns.	

PRACTICE 2

Cross out the mistake in each sentence and write the correct possessive pronoun: *mine, yours, his, hers, ours,* or *theirs*. The first one has been done for you.

1. Your children are grown up, but ~~my~~ mine are still young.

2. Your son has his friends, and your daughter has her.

3. This old car is our's.

4. My neighbors' dogs are huge, but mines are small.

5. My dogs are poodles, and their are German shepherds.

6. That is not my problem. It is your's!

Answers start on page 171.

REFLEXIVE PRONOUNS

See for Yourself

Look in the mirror, and what do you see?
I see **myself**.

INSIGHT

In the second sentence, *see* is the verb. What is the subject? _____ What is the object?
_____ You're right if you said that the word *I* is the subject and *myself* is the object.

Do the words *I* and *myself* refer to the same person or to different people? _____
Both words refer to the same person. The word *myself* is called a ***reflexive pronoun***.

> **When the subject of the sentence and the object pronoun refer to the same person (or thing), use a reflexive pronoun for the object.**

Pronoun	Example
myself	I can see **myself**.
yourself	Lonnie, you hurt **yourself**.
himself herself itself	She was talking to **herself**.
ourselves	We made the cake for **ourselves**.
yourselves	Both of you hurt **yourselves**.
themselves	They gave **themselves** raises.

Remember that the pronoun *you* can be used when talking about one person (singular) or many people (plural). Be careful! When talking about one person, use the reflexive *yourself*. When talking about more than one person, use the reflexive *yourselves*.

What is wrong with these two sentences?

He said so hisself.
Mattie and Edric mailed the letters to theirselves.

Are the words *hisself* and *theirselves* in the chart? No! Be sure to use the correct words: *himself* and *themselves*.

He said so **himself**.
Mattie and Edric mailed the letters to **themselves**.

PRACTICE

Read each question carefully. Then answer the question, using a reflexive correctly in each statement. The first one has been done for you.

1. Who are you looking at?

   I _am looking at myself._____

2. Who is Isabel talking to?

   She _____

3. Who are the children drawing pictures of?

   The children _____

4. Who are you and Sally shopping for?

   Sally and I _____

5. Who is Irving taking a picture of?

   He _____

6. Who are John and I working for?

   You _____

7. Who is the dog scratching?

   It _____

Answers start on page 172.

CUMULATIVE REVIEW

Show What You Know

As you do these exercises, keep in mind everything you have learned about possessives.

PROOFREAD

Read this passage, paying special attention to the possessives and plurals. Find and correct the mistakes. Cross out each mistake and write the correct word above it. There are seventeen mistakes in all, and the first one has been done for you.

At holiday time, my neighborhood looks like a carnival. In December,
my next-door ~~neighbors'~~ **neighbors** put colored light's in theirs windows. Across the street, the Robinson's yard is decorated with two Santa's and one giant reindeer. The reindeers' nose is a bright red lightbulb, and it's tail is a white lightbulb. Down the block, Mrs. Smiths' roof is covered with Santa Claus, Santas sleigh, and several yellow star's. The fat elf by the driveway is her's, too. The Hendersons front yard has a huge Christmas tree. Everyone else has a regular green tree, but their's is pink and white! Mine apartment is very plain. Other peoples' windows are full of lights and tinsel, but mines just have curtains. I guess that is why my neighbor's call me Mr. Scrooge!

Answers start on page 172.

WRITING ASSIGNMENT

Think of a famous person—a movie or TV star, a singer or musician, a sports star, or a politician or leader. Write a paragraph of about six sentences about the person's family and about the things he or she owns. (If you don't know these details, you may invent them!) In your paragraph, include as many possessives as possible. Use both possessive nouns and possessive pronouns.

When you are finished, proofread your paragraph.

- ☑ Verb tenses are correct.
- ☑ All possessive nouns are punctuated correctly.
- ☑ All possessive pronouns are used correctly.
- ☑ Cross out apostrophes that don't belong.

CHAPTER 6
ADJECTIVES AND ADVERBS

- To understand what an adjective is and how it is used
- To understand what an adverb is and how it is used
- To understand and use comparatives and superlatives correctly

ADJECTIVES

The Beautiful People

Jessica is **beautiful**.

INSIGHT

Look at the **boldface** word, and use it to answer the question. What is Jessica like? _____ The word *beautiful* is an **adjective**. An adjective tells what someone or something is like. Look at another sentence.

Jessica is a **good** actress.

Use the **boldface** word to answer this question. What kind of actress is Jessica? _____ The word *good* is another adjective. Besides telling what someone or something is like, adjectives can also answer the question "What kind?" In other words, adjectives are words that describe.

In the first sentence, the word *beautiful* describes *Jessica*. In the second sentence, *good* describes *actress*. What kind of words are *Jessica* and *actress*? (circle one)   **a.** nouns **b.** verbs.   You're right if you said that they are nouns.

Adjectives can also describe pronouns, as in the sentence *She is beautiful*. Here the word *beautiful* describes the pronoun *she*.

> **Adjectives are words that describe nouns or pronouns.**

79

PRACTICE 1

The adjectives in these sentences are in **boldface**. Draw an arrow from the adjective to the noun or pronoun it describes. (Be careful. Your arrows will not always go in the same direction.) The first one has been done for you.

1. Jessica is a **good** actress.
2. She is **beautiful**.
3. Robert is **handsome**.
4. He is a **famous** actor.

5. He looks **sensational**
6. Robert is a **rich** man.
7. Do you know any **real** actors?

Answers start on page 172.

PRACTICE 2

Now try to think of your own adjectives. Write three adjectives for each question.

1. Think of an actress. What adjectives could describe her?

   _____

2. Think of a wrestler. What adjectives could describe him or her?

   _____

3. Think of a homeless person. What adjectives could describe him or her?

   _____

4. Think of someone who has just won a lottery. What adjectives could describe him or her? _____

PRACTICE 3

Now write sentences using adjectives. Think of five people you know. You may include friends, relatives, neighbors, coworkers, your boss, or anyone else. Write a complete sentence describing each with an adjective.

EXAMPLES: My cousin is **tall**.
My **rude** boss smokes cigars.

PRACTICE 4

Rewrite each sentence by adding an adjective before the noun. Use a different adjective in each sentence. Be sure to change *a* or *an* if necessary. The first one has been done for you.

1. That is a building. That is an old building.
2. I want a house.
3. Janet is a singer.
4. Charles is an actor.

5. We saw a movie.
6. I heard a song.
7. They read a book.

Answers will vary.

ADVERBS

Oh, Really?

Mark speaks **softly**, and he listens **carefully**.

INSIGHT

Look at the sentence above, and answer the questions.

How does Mark speak? _____

How does Mark listen? _____

The words *softly* and *carefully* are called ***adverbs***. They answer the question "How?" In other words, they tell how the action of the verb is done. Now look at the last two letters of the adverbs *softly* and *carefully*. What are they? __ __

> **Adverbs tell how the action of the verb is done.**
> **Adverbs usually end in *ly*.**

PRACTICE 1

Underline each adverb. Then draw an arrow from the adverb to the verb it describes. Be careful. The adverb may come before or after the verb. The first one has been done for you.

1. Mark speaks softly to his children.

2. He carefully listens to their problems.

3. He clearly explains the rules.

4. The children look at their father respectfully.

5. They answer him politely.

6. Most of the time, they happily obey him.

Answers start on page 172.

Spelling

You may have noticed that an adverb looks something like an adjective with the letters *ly* on the end. For example, take the adjective *soft*, add *ly*, and you get *softly*. Try some others:

clear + ly = _____   polite + ly = _____

careful + ly = _____   respectful + ly = _____

Notice that the letter *l* appears twice in *carefully* and *respectfully*.

As you can see, you don't usually need to make any spelling changes when adding *ly* to an adjective. However, there is one spelling change you must learn. Look at this example:

happ<u>y</u> + ly = happ<u>ily</u>

The *y* in *happy* changes to the letter ____. Try some more examples:

lazy + ly = _____   sleepy + ly = _____

Most adverbs are spelled ADJECTIVE + *ly*.
If an adjective ends in *y*, change *y* to *i* before adding *ly*.

PRACTICE 2

Answer each question using the correct adverb. Look at the adjective in parentheses and change it to an adverb by adding *ly*. The first one has been done for you.

1. How does Stella treat her children? (*unkind*)

   Stella treats her children unkindly.

2. How does she speak to her children? (*nasty*)

3. How do the children talk to her? (*rude*)

4. How do the children look at their mother? (*disrespectful*)

5. How do the children behave? (*bad*)

6. How do the children fight? (*noisy*)

Answers start on page 172.

Irregular Adverbs

Sometimes children behave badly.
Other times they behave well.

Each sentence above has an adverb. What is the adverb in the first sentence? _____ What is the adverb in the second sentence? _____ You are right if you wrote *badly* for the first sentence and *well* for the second. Adverbs like *well* are called **irregular adverbs** because they do not end in *ly*.

Some adverbs do not end in *ly*.

Here are some irregular adverbs.

well   fast   hard*

PRACTICE 3

Answer the questions about yourself. Use different adverbs—regular or irregular—in your answers. The first one has been done for you.

1. How do you walk? __I walk slowly.__

2. How do you speak?

3. How do you listen to people in your family?

4. How do you read?

5. How do you write?

6. How do you treat your friends?

7. How do you dance?

8. How do you cook?

9. How do you drive?

10. How do you work?

Answers will vary.

---

*Note: The word *hardly* has a different meaning from *hard*. *Hardly* means *barely* or *scarcely*. *Hard* can be either an adjective or an adverb.

Another Use for Adverbs

That idea is completely crazy.

Look for the adverb in the sentence above and write it here: _____ What word is this adverb, *completely*, describing? It tells more about the word *crazy*. (How crazy is the idea? Just a little crazy? No—completely crazy!) The adverb *completely* tells more about the adjective *crazy*.

> **Adverbs can tell more about adjectives.**

PRACTICE 4

Each sentence below has an adjective. Rewrite the sentence, adding an adverb before the adjective to tell more about the adjective. Here are some adverbs you could use: *completely, extremely, strangely, unusually, happily, insanely*. The first one has been done for you.

1. Phil and Janet were married. Phil and Janet were happily married.
2. They were honest with each other.
3. One day, Phil was silent at the dinner table.
4. He was nervous, too.
5. Janet was upset by this.
6. It turned out that Phil was jealous.

Answers will vary.

ADJECTIVE OR ADVERB?

Real Nice or Really Nice?

My grandmother was **nice**.
My grandmother always treated me **nicely**.

INSIGHT

Look at the two sentences above. The writer has used the word *nice* in one sentence and *nicely* in the other. Is *nice* an adjective or an adverb? _____ How about *nicely*? _____ You are right if you saw that *nice* is an adjective and *nicely* is an adverb.

Now remember what an adjective does. An adjective describes a noun or a pronoun. In the first sentence, what word does *nice* describe? _____ You're right if you said it describes the noun *grandmother*. It answers the question "What kind of grandmother was she?"

Remember what an adverb does. An adverb tells about the action of the verb. In the second sentence, what does *nicely* describe? _____ You are correct if you wrote that *nicely* tells about the verb *treated*. It answers the question "How did your grandmother treat you?"

Be careful! Don't write an adjective when you need an adverb. The sentences below are incorrect. How can they be fixed?

> She was real nice. She always treated me kind.

To fix the first sentence, *real* should be changed to _____.

To fix the second sentence, *kind* should be changed to _____.

> She was **really** nice. (*Use an adverb to tell "How nice?"*)
> She always treated me **kindly**. (*Use an adverb to tell "How did she treat you?"*)

PRACTICE 1

Look at the **boldface** words in the sentences below. Some are adjectives, and some are adverbs.

- Draw an arrow from the boldface word to the word it tells about.
- Circle ADJ. for an adjective and ADV. for an adverb.

The first one has been done for you.

1. Mrs. Stone is a **good** person.   (ADJ.)   ADV.

2. She speaks **kindly**.   ADJ.   ADV.

3. She is **polite**.   ADJ.   ADV.

4. She treats people **politely**.   ADJ.   ADV.

5. Mrs. Stone is **really** thoughtful.   ADJ.   ADV.

6. Mrs. Stone is a **careful** listener.   ADJ.   ADV.

7. She is a **good** singer.   ADJ.   ADV.

8. She sings **well**.   ADJ.   ADV.

Answers start on page 172.

PRACTICE 2

Rewrite each sentence, adding an adjective or adverb correctly. Try to use different adjectives and different adverbs. The first two have been done for you.

1. I am a cook. _I am a messy cook._   5. I drive.

2. I cook. _I cook marvelously._   6. I am a driver.

3. I am a dancer.   7. I speak.

4. I dance.   8. I am a speaker.

Answers will vary.

PROOFREAD

Find and correct the mistakes with adjectives and adverbs. Cross out a wrong word and write the correct one above it. There are eight mistakes in all, and the first one has been done for you.

My parents left when I was ~~real~~ *really* young, so I lived with my grandmother.

She took good care of me, and she raised me good. She had a real quiet

voice, and she always talked to me soft. I liked to listen to her because

she always spoke to me serious, but she was never unkind. I lived happy

with her until I grew up. She peaceful died a few years ago, but I still

remember her good.

Answers start on page 172.

COMPARATIVES

The Bigger the Better

New York is bigger than Los Angeles.
New York is also more crowded.
Los Angeles is smoggier, though.

INSIGHT

Look at the three sentences above. The writer is making a comparison in each sentence. How many cities are being compared here? _____ Each sentence is comparing the two cities New York and Los Angeles.

Now take a look at the adjectives in the three sentences. Write them here: _____, more _____, _____. Check your answers. Did you write *bigger, more crowded*, and *smoggier*? These are called **comparatives** because they are used to compare two things.

> **Comparative adjectives are used to compare two people, places, things, or ideas.**

Comparatives with *er*

Read these adjectives out loud: small, large, short, long, tall, cheap, old, new. Each of these words is very short. To make the comparative form of these short adjectives, just add the letters *er*. Try it:

small + er = _____   new + er = _____

short + er = _____   long + er = _____

What are the comparative forms for *tall, cheap,* and *old?*

Look at one of these comparative adjectives in a sentence:

Baltimore is smaller than New York.

Write the word that appears after *smaller* here: _____. Notice that this word, *than*, is not the same as the word *then*.

SPELLING

When you add *er* to adjectives, follow the same spelling rules as when you add *ed* to verbs. Double the final consonant of words ending in one vowel and one consonant, as in this example: *big—bigger*. For words that end in silent *e*, just add *r: large—larger*.

Comparatives with *ier*

Study these adjectives: windy, rainy, happy, funny, heavy, sleepy, lazy. What do all of these adjectives have in common? They all end in the letter *y*. To change these to the comparative form, change the *y* to *i* and add *er*. Try it:

windy + er = _____   rainy + er = _____

happy + er = _____   funny + er = _____

What are the comparative forms of *heavy*, *sleepy*, and *lazy*?

Irregular Comparatives

The comparative forms for *good* and *bad* are irregular:

Adjective	Comparative Form	Example
good	better	Stevie Wonder's new song is **good,** but his old hit is **better**.
bad	worse	You feel **bad,** but I feel **worse** than you.

PRACTICE 1

Write a sentence comparing each pair of cities. Put *er* on the end of the adjective according to the spelling rules, and use *than*. The first one has been done for you.

1. Baltimore/New York—small $\underline{Baltimore\ is\ smaller\ than\ New\ York.}$

2. New York/Chicago—large

3. Los Angeles/New York—sunny

4. Vancouver/Los Angeles—rainy

5. Miami/New York—hot

6. Phoenix/Boston—new

7. Los Angeles/Kansas City—smoggy

8. (*The place where you live*)/
   (*Pick another city*)—good

Answers start on page 172.

Comparatives with *More*

Say these adjectives out loud: responsible, beautiful, polluted, interesting, unusual, intelligent. Each of these adjectives is long. It would be too awkward to pronounce these words with *er* added to the ends of them. (Try saying *responsibler*!) So instead, just put the word *more* before the adjective—for example, *more beautiful* and *more intelligent*.

PRACTICE 2

Write sentences comparing the cities below. Use *more* before the adjective, and use the word *than*. The first one has been done for you.

1. New York/Santa Fe—crowded <u>New York is more crowded than Santa Fe.</u>

2. Chicago/Santa Fe—polluted

3. Boston/Dallas—historic

4. New York/Spokane—famous

5. Detroit/Miami—industrial

6. Miami/Toronto—tropical

Answers start on page 172.

A Common Problem

Watch out for a common problem. Can you find the mistakes in the sentences below?

> Chicago is more smaller than New York.
> It is more windier, though.

What word should be taken out of each sentence? _____ You're right if you said that *more* does not belong in the sentences. If the word already has *er* or *ier* at the end, do not use *more*.

Do not use *more* before a word with the *er* or *ier* ending.

PROOFREAD

Find and correct the errors in regular and irregular comparatives. Cross out any wrong word. If necessary, write the correct form above it. There are six mistakes in all, and the first mistake has been corrected for you.

> Let's compare two cities: Toronto and Las Vegas. First, Toronto's
>
> weather is ~~worser~~ worse than the weather in Las Vegas. It is much more colder
>
> and snowyer than Las Vegas. In cultural life, Toronto is famouser for its
>
> museums and concerts. Las Vegas is more smaller then Toronto, but if
>
> you like gambling, it is a more better place to be.

Answers start on page 172.

PRACTICE 3

Think of two towns or cities—your own and another one. Write six sentences comparing these two cities. Use the correct comparative forms of different adjectives. In your last sentence, be sure to say which city you think is better.

Answers will vary.

SUPERLATIVES

The Best Is Yet to Come

New York is the **biggest** city in the United States.
It is also the **most crowded.**
It isn't the **windiest**, though.

INSIGHT

The sentences above are talking about New York—one city out of many in the United States. The sentences show how New York stands out from all the other cities. To do this, the writer uses the *superlative* form of the adjective. Superlatives show how one person, place, thing, or group is different from all the rest. Remember, use comparatives (*smaller, wider*) when comparing just two things. Use superlatives (*smallest, widest*) when you are talking about a group of three or more.

Look now at the superlative forms in the sentences above. Write each superlative below next to the adjective form.

Adjective	Superlative
big	the _____
crowded	the _____ _____
windy	the _____

Do the superlative forms remind you of the comparative forms? In fact, they follow very similar rules. See if you can guess them.

Add *est* to _____ words.

Use *most* with _____ words.

If a word ends in _____, change *y* to *i* and add *est*.

Remember to use the word *the* at the beginning.

Type of Word	What to Do	Examples
Short words	Add *est*	the tall<u>est</u>
Words that end in *y*	Change *y* to *iest*	the wind<u>iest</u>
Long words	Use *most*	the <u>most</u> crowded

> **Superlative adjectives show how one person, place, thing, or idea stands out from all the rest.**

Irregular Superlatives

Just like the comparatives, the superlatives for *good* and *bad* are also irregular:

Adjective	Superlative	Example
good	the best	Of the three basketball players, he was the **best.**
bad	the worst	This was the **worst** day of my life.

PRACTICE 1

Write a sentence about each city. Use the superlative form of the adjective. The first one has been done for you.

1. Chicago—windy <u>Chicago is the windiest city.</u>

2. New York—large   6. Seattle—rainy

3. Phoenix—sunny   7. (choose a city)—good

4. Philadelphia—historic   8. (choose a city)—bad

5. Detroit—industrial

Answers start on page 173.

Common Problems

Watch out for the spelling of two words. Always remember that both *best* and *worst* end in the letters *st*. Can you correct this sentence?

He is the bes singer but the worse dancer in our crowd.

You're right if you changed *bes* and *worse* to *best* and *worst*. Be careful about one more point. Do not use *most* with superlatives ending in *est*. Can you correct this sentence?

That is the most tallest building in the world.

You are right if you crossed out the word *most*.

> **Do not use *most* with a superlative adjective ending in *est* or *iest*.**

PRACTICE 2

Think of ten people you know. What makes each different from all the rest? Write a sentence about each of these people using the superlative forms of the adjectives below. (Watch out for special forms!) The first two have been done for you.

1. tall—man <u>Sam is the tallest man I know.</u>
2. intelligent—student <u>Sheila is the most intelligent student.</u>

3. smart—man   8. serious—person

4. interesting—person   9. funny—person

5. good—dancer   10. fast—talker

6. bad—singer   11. sympathetic—listener

7. happy—child   12. brave—person

Answers will vary.

Review

Review what you have learned about comparative and superlative adjective forms. Remember that comparatives are used to compare *two* people, places, things, or ideas. Superlatives show how one person, place, thing, or idea is different from all the rest—there must be at least three people or things to use the superlative.

PRACTICE 3

Fill in the correct comparative and superlative forms of each adjective. Watch out for the irregular forms. The first one has been done for you.

Adjective	Comparative	Superlative
1. tall	taller	the tallest
2. pretty		
3. beautiful		
4. strong		
5. surprising		
6. chubby		
7. good		
8. bad		

PROOFREAD

Find and correct the errors in this paragraph. There are eight mistakes in all, and the first one has been done for you.

I have three sisters. Jackie is the ~~most~~ oldest. She is also the more musical of all three. Meg is the most youngest. In some ways, she is intelligenter than Jackie. She is the bestest student of all, but she is the worse cook. Wilga is a more better cook than Meg. Each sister has something she does the bes.

Answers start on page 173.

CUMULATIVE REVIEW

Show What You Know

What do you look for when you are shopping for something? Quality? Price? Size? Appearance? All of these can be important. Now imagine that you just got a big bonus, and you are going shopping for a used car.

WRITING ASSIGNMENT

At the used car dealer, you see three cars lined up: a Mercedes, a Cadillac, and a Ford Escort. Look carefully at the cars, their ages, their prices, and their mileage.

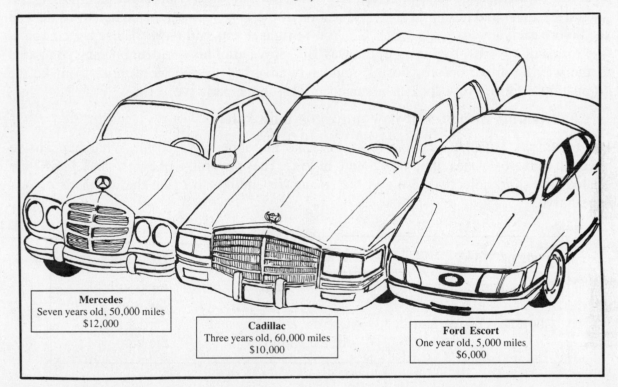

Mercedes
Seven years old, 50,000 miles
$12,000

Cadillac
Three years old, 60,000 miles
$10,000

Ford Escort
One year old, 5,000 miles
$6,000

Before deciding which one to get, you need to compare the different cars. You'll need to answer questions like these: Which car is the most expensive? Which has lower mileage—the Cadillac or the Ford?

Write at least ten sentences comparing the different cars. You will need to use superlative adjectives to tell how one car is different from the rest. You'll need comparative adjectives to compare one car to another. Some adjectives you might want to use are *expensive, cheap, large, small, roomy, low, high, old, new, elegant, classy, practical*, and *economical*. At the end, tell which car you will buy.

EXAMPLES: The Mercedes is the most expensive car.
 The Ford's mileage is lower than the Cadillac's mileage.

When you are finished, remember to proofread your work. Check for the following:

☑ You have used comparatives and superlatives correctly.
☑ Apostrophes are used correctly on all possessive nouns.
☑ You have used the correct verb forms.

COMPARING WITH ADVERBS

Seeing More Clearly

After the accident, Biff drove more safely than before.
He drove more slowly and watched more carefully.

INSIGHT

Read the sentences above. Notice the three adverbs and write them here: _____,
_____, and _____. But look at the sentences again. What word do you
see before each adverb? _____ You're right if you said *more*. These are comparative forms of adverbs. In this case, the way Biff drove after his accident is being compared
to the way he drove before. For all regular *ly* adverbs, use the word *more* to make the
comparative form. Now look at a sentence with the superlative form.

Of all his friends, Biff now drove **the most safely**.

For regular *ly* adverbs, use *the most* to make the superlative form. What happens to
irregular adverbs (ones that don't end in *ly*)? These words—like *fast* and *hard*—are
treated like short adjectives, so add the *er* and *est* endings to make the comparative and
superlative.

Type of Word	What to Do	Examples
Most adverbs ending in *ly*	Use *more* and *the most*	**more** safely **the most** safely
Short adverbs without *ly*	Use the *er* ending and the *est* ending	hard<u>er</u> the hard<u>est</u>

There are also some irregular forms to learn:

Adverb	Comparative	Superlative
well	better	the best
badly	worse	the worst
far	farther	the farthest

PRACTICE

Write the correct comparative and superlative adverb forms on each line of the passage below. The first one has been done for you.

Before the accident, Biff drove the ____**worst**____ (*badly*) of anyone he knew. He drove dangerously, and he loved showing off. One night,
his friend Sally challenged him to a race. She bet that she could drive
_____ (*fast*) than he could. They took off down the road at
70 miles per hour. At first, Sally was driving _____
(*recklessly*) than Biff. Then Mike joined the race, and he stepped even
_____ (*hard*) on the gas. Biff laughed at the others and thought
he would soon prove that he could drive the _____ (*well*) and the
_____ (*fast*) of them all. But before he knew what happened, he
crashed head-on into a tree.

After six months in the hospital, Biff still couldn't walk well. After
a year, he began to walk _____ (*well*) than before. Then he got
a new car. The first day on the road, Biff drove _____
(*cautiously*) than he had ever driven before. In fact, of all his friends, he
now drove _____ (*carefully*).

PROOFREAD

Keep in mind all you have learned about comparative and superlative forms of adjectives and adverbs. (You may want to review the rule boxes on pages 88, 90, and 94.)

Find and correct the errors in this paragraph. Cross out the wrong form. If necessary, write the correct form above. There are eleven mistakes in all, and the first one has been corrected for you.

Biff's life was ~~difficulter~~ *more difficult* after the accident. He had to walk much
more slowlier than before. He couldn't do his old job, and his new job
was much badder than the old one. He became much seriouser, and some
of his friends deserted him. But in some ways his life became more better.
Before the accident, he was the most fastest driver of all his friends. After-
wards, he became the most safest. He used to act without thinking, but
now he thought more carefuller before he acted. He began to behave more
maturer. Even though his life was more harder, he decided he would always
try his bestest.

Answers start on page 173.

CUMULATIVE REVIEW

Show What You Know

Right now, you may be working for someone, but someday you might be the boss. Imagine that you are the manager for the office of a big department store. Three workers are up for promotion to the position of secretary. You can pick only one. You want to choose the best person for the job. Study the information about each worker.

Ms. Jones
- age 24
- great sense of humor
- polite
- types 40 words per minute
- dresses casually
- works fairly hard

Ms. Teeter
- age 35
- good sense of humor
- very polite
- types 50 words per minute
- dresses formally
- works very hard

Mr. Lifton
- age 30
- no sense of humor
- rude
- types 65 words per minute
- dresses very formally
- works very, very hard

It is hard to make up your mind, so you decide to write down some sentences comparing the three workers. Write ten sentences. Talk about what makes each worker different from the others. Compare two workers to each other. Use the comparative and superlative forms of adjectives and adverbs correctly. Remember to use the correct verb forms, too. Finally, tell which worker you are going to promote.

EXAMPLES: Ms. Jones is the youngest.
Ms. Jones types more slowly than Mr. Lifton.

When you are finished, be sure to proofread your work. Check for the following:

☑ All your comparative and superlative adjectives and adverbs are used correctly.
☑ Apostrophes are in the correct places on all possessive nouns.
☑ You have used the correct verb forms.

CHAPTER 7 AGREEMENT

Goals

- To use the correct form of a verb with its subject
- To use the correct form of a verb with a compound subject
- To avoid double subjects
- To use the correct form of a verb when the subject and verb are separated
- To use the correct form of a verb with tricky subjects and noncount nouns
- To locate the subject and use the correct verb form when the sentence begins with *Here* or *There*.

Review of Subjects and Verbs

Refresh your memory about verbs and subjects. The word that tells the *action* of a sentence is the _____. (It can also tell what someone or something is.) The word that tells *who* or *what* is doing the action of the verb is the _____.

Locating the Subject

As you know, the subject and the verb are sometimes right next to each other. At other times, the subject and verb are separated by other words. These other words may tell more about the subject or the verb, but they are not part of either one. Look at these examples:

> My son often helps with the housework.
> Those children over there are my daughter's.

In the first sentence, *helps* is the verb and *son* is the subject. The word *often* just tells when he helps with the housework. In the second sentence, the word *are* is the verb and *children* is the subject.

PRACTICE

Underline the verb in each sentence. Label the word or words with a *V*. Then find the subject—ask yourself who or what is doing the action of the verb. Underline the subject and label it with an *S*. The first one has been done for you.

1. I am working hard on the kitchen walls.

2. Every day, I scrape away a little more grease.

3. My family helps me.

4. They don't fry anything on the stove anymore.

5. They really are making an effort to clean this place.

6. This morning my son was scrubbing the floor for a while.

7. I sometimes wonder about all this dirt.

8. The range hood over there has five years of grease on it.

9. It didn't bother us until last week.

10. Then my mother came for a visit.

Answers start on page 173.

BASIC AGREEMENT

Let's Agree on Something

She live in Nashville. She don't like country music.

INSIGHT

Can you spot the mistakes? What is wrong with the words? Instead of *live*, it should be
_____. Instead of *don't like*, it should be _____. (Check your
answers: *lives* and *doesn't like*.)

The problem with these sentences is that the verbs don't agree with the subjects. **Subject-verb agreement** means that the verb form is right for the subject. You have already
studied, in Chapters 3 and 4, which verb forms go with which subjects. Take some time
now to review this information on pages 32–57.

> **Be sure that your verbs agree with your subjects.**

PRACTICE

Show what you remember. Write the correct form of the verb on the line. Make sure
your verbs agree with your subjects.

1. (*live/lives*) She _____ in Nashville.

2. (*don't/doesn't*) She _____ like country music.

3. (*am/is*) I _____ living in Houston.

4. (*don't/doesn't*) I _____ like Texas barbecue.

5. (*are/is*) They _____ from Boston.

6. (*drink/drinks*) They almost never _____ tea.

7. (*are/is*) Terrence _____ working in a donut shop.

8. (*don't/doesn't*) He _____ like donuts.

9. (*was/were*) We _____ in Colorado last winter.

10. (*don't/doesn't*) We _____ like skiing.

11. (*was/were*) Mattie _____ at the bar last night.

12. (*wasn't/weren't*) She certainly _____ drinking.

Answers start on page 173.

COMPOUND SUBJECTS

The King and I

Ryan **is** sick. He **needs** a doctor.
Ryan and I **are** sick. Ryan and I **need** a doctor.

INSIGHT

In the top line, the verbs *is* and *needs* agree with the subjects *Ryan* and *He*. Now look at the second line. The verbs in those sentences are *are* and *need*. What are the subjects of both these sentences? _____ You're correct if you saw that the phrase *Ryan and I* is the subject of both sentences. The phrase *Ryan and I* is an example of a **compound subject**. A compound subject is made of two or more subjects joined by the word *and*.

Compound subjects are always plural and always need the verb form that goes with a plural subject. Think of *Ryan and I* as another way of saying *we*. Try these other examples of compound subjects:

1. Ryan and I = _____

2. Ryan and Jane = _____

3. He and I = _____

4. He and you = _____

You should have written (1) *we*, (2) *they*, (3) *we*, and (4) *you*.

Use the verb form for plural subjects with compound subjects.

Sometimes a compound subject includes more than two subjects. In this case you must use a comma to separate the parts of the subject. Draw circles around the commas in this example:

Ryan, Jane, and I are sick.

When there are three or more subjects, use a comma after each subject that comes before the word *and*.

Do not use a comma after the last part of a subject.

INCORRECT: Ryan, Jane, and I, caught a cold.
CORRECT: Ryan, Jane, and I caught a cold.

PRACTICE 1

All of these sentences have compound subjects. If the compound subject has three or more items, add commas in the correct places. If the subject has only two items, write *no comma* on the line. The first one has been done for you.

no comma 1. Ryan and I are sick.

_____ 2. Ryan Jane and I need a doctor.

_____ 3. Jane and I have the flu.

_____ 4. My head my ears and my throat hurt.

_____ 5. Cold weather bad food and a late night caused us to get sick.

_____ 6. The doctor and the nurse want to see us.

PRACTICE 2

Combine these sentences to make sentences with compound subjects.

- Use the word *and* correctly.
- Remember to use commas only when there are three or more subjects.
- Check your verb forms carefully!

The first one has been done for you.

1. Ryan looks bad. I look bad. **Ryan and I look bad.**

2. Ryan needs a doctor. Jane needs a doctor. I need a doctor.

3. Ryan is coughing. Jane is coughing. I am coughing.

4. Pills are expensive. Vitamins are expensive. Cough syrup is expensive.

5. Children get sick easily. Old people get sick easily.

6. Good nutrition is important for sick people. Bed rest is important for sick people.

Answers start on page 173.

Compound Subjects with Pronouns

Be extra careful when you use a pronoun in a compound subject. Which is the correct pronoun?

Ryan and (*I? me?*) are sick.

You are correct if you said *I*. The word *I* is a subject pronoun. Only subject pronouns can be used in a compound subject.

Can you remember the subject pronouns? Write them here: _____
_____ If you need to refresh your memory, look back to page 28 for a list. The correct subject pronoun *I* is used in the next sentence. However, there is another problem. Look at the sentence:

I and Ryan are sick.

The word order is mixed up. The pronoun *I* should be last, not first. The writer should have begun with *Ryan and I.*

> Ryan and I are sick.

Use a subject pronoun in a compound subject.
The pronoun *I* comes last in a compound subject.

PRACTICE 3

If the sentence uses pronouns correctly, write *OK* in the blank. If there is a mistake, correct it. The first one has been corrected for you.

_____ 1. Ryan, Jane, and ~~me~~ I stayed out too late last weekend.

_____ 2. Jane and he didn't eat properly.

_____ 3. I and Ryan had too much to drink.

_____ 4. Me and my brother stayed out until dawn.

_____ 5. Him and me didn't get home until six in the morning.

_____ 6. He and I woke up our sister by mistake.

_____ 7. Our parents and her got angry with us.

_____ 8. Them and my grandmother were worried about us.

_____ 9. My brother and I just wanted to rest.

Answers start on page 173.

AVOIDING DOUBLE SUBJECTS

Double Trouble

My brother he plays the guitar well.

INSIGHT

What is wrong with the sentence above? To find the problem, first look for the verb and write it here: _____ Now, what is the subject? That is hard to answer because there are two subjects—*brother* and *he*! However, this is not a compound subject because both words refer to the same person. *My brother he* is a **double subject**—two words for only one subject. If you have written a double subject, take out one of them. Here is how the corrected sentence looks:

My brother plays the guitar well.

Don't use a double subject.

It's OK to use the person's name after his or her description, like this:

My sister Jill embroiders well.

Here the writer is not using a double subject but is using the name to tell *which* sister.

PROOFREAD

Read the passage and watch out for the mistakes with double subjects. Cross out any unnecessary words. There are four mistakes in all, and the first one has been done for you.

My brother Joe plays guitar in a band. He also sings back-up.

The other band members ~~they~~ sing too. Of course, the band members they

also play their instruments—keyboard, bass, and drums. The drummer he

is very talented. He and my brother they want to start a new band together.

Answers start on page 174.

PRACTICE

Think about six people you know. Make a list of these people. Don't use their names. Instead, write *My sister, My boss,* and so on. Be sure to include a few plurals like *parents, cousins,* or *classmates.* Now write a sentence about each. Be careful not to write a double subject by mistake.

WRONG: My sister she is a good basketball player.
RIGHT: My sister is a good basketball player.

Answers will vary.

INTERRUPTING PHRASES

Separation Anxiety

A mother with triplets (*has? have?*) her hands full.

INSIGHT

Which verb is correct for the sentence above? To answer that, first you must find the subject. There are two nouns in this sentence: *mother* and *triplets*. Only one is the subject. To find out, ask yourself "*Who* has her hands full—the mother or the triplets?" _____ You're right if you said the mother has her hands full. The phrase *with triplets* just tells you more about the mother's situation. Look at the sentences below with the phrase *with triplets* crossed out to see which verb makes the most sense.

A mother ~~with triplets~~ **have** her hands full.
A mother ~~with triplets~~ **has** her hands full.

If you said *has*, you were right. *Has*, not *have*, is the correct verb form when the subject is a singular noun.

A mother with triplets **has** her hands full.

> **Sometimes the subject and verb are separated by a phrase.**
> **Make sure the verb agrees with the subject, not the phrase.**

PRACTICE 1

Find the subject and the verb in each sentence, and label each with *S* or *V*. Cross out the interrupting phrase in between. (Note: All of the sentences are correct.) The first one has been done for you.

1. A mother ~~with triplets~~ has her hands full.   [S ... V labels shown above]

2. A father with five children is always busy.

3. The baby of the family is sometimes spoiled.

4. Sometimes parents of teenagers are not strict enough.

5. Teenagers in a large family usually want more privacy.

6. The people next door to me have teenage triplets.

7. The boys next door share one room.

8. One of them goes to a special school.

PRACTICE 2

Underline the subject of each sentence. Then choose the correct verb. The first one has been done for you.

1. (*have/had*) <u>Parents</u> of any child **have** a big responsibility.

2. (*are/is*) A child with loving parents _____ lucky.

3. (*need/needs*) Most children with special problems _____ special care.

4. (*are/is*) Often, the parents of a disabled child _____ not prepared for the expense.

5. (*have/has*) A teacher of retarded children _____ to be patient.

6. (*require/requires*) A program for children with special problems _____ help from the parents.

Answers start on page 174.

A Common Problem

What is wrong with this sentence?

Children with special problems they need extra help.

To find out, first find the verb of the sentence—*need*. Is the subject *they*? No, it can't be—the sentence reads *Children . . . need extra help. Children* is the subject. Both *children* and *they* refer to the same people, so there is a double subject here. To fix the problem, take away the word *they*.

Children with special problems need extra help.

**Remember not to write a double subject.
Be extra careful when a phrase separates the subject and verb.**

PRACTICE 3

Each sentence has a double subject. Cross out the unnecessary pronoun. The first one has been done for you.

1. The child next door ~~she~~ is deaf.

2. The parents of this little girl they love her very much.

3. The mother of the family she speaks sign language well.

4. The father of the family he is trying to learn it.

5. The school in the neighborhood it has special classes for deaf children.

6. The teacher of one of these classes he is helping the parents.

Answers start on page 174.

PRACTICE 4

Think about people and places in your community, then complete the following sentences. Be sure the verbs agree with the subjects. Don't write double subjects. The first one has been done for you.

1. The people in my neighborhood . . . **The people in my neighborhood are friendly.**

2. The people next door . . .

3. The teenage daughter of some friends . . .

4. The building across from me . . .

5. The door to my house . . .

6. The stores in my area . . .

7. The food in the local supermarkets . . .

8. The cars on my street . . .

Answers will vary.

PROOFREAD

Review what you have learned so far about subject-verb agreement. Find and correct the errors in verb forms in the paragraph below. There are thirteen errors in all, and the first one has been corrected for you.

Crime in the streets ~~are~~ **is** a serious problem in modern cities. Robberies, rapes, and muggings happens every day. Experts give different reasons for crime.

Unemployment in the cities are certainly a major cause. People without a job does not have enough money. In addition, they are angry and frustrated. Often, anger and frustration leads to crime.

Gangs is another problem. Young men and even young women joins gangs because they have no other choice. A gang of boys force another boy to join by threatening to kill him. Fights between one gang and another is responsible for much crime in the street.

Sometimes violence in the home causes crime on the streets. A child of violent parents learn to be violent himself. Beatings and other kinds of violent punishment teaches a child that it is OK to hurt other people.

Crime in the streets hurt everyone. To stop it, the schools, the government, and the family needs to work together.

Answers start on page 174.

TRICKY SUBJECTS

Everything and Nothing

In this section, we will be looking at subjects that can be tricky. First, we will look at pronouns and other subjects that are always singular. Then we will look at some nouns that are always plural. Finally, we will see how to make noncount nouns agree with their verbs.

Subjects That Are Always Singular

Don't do that. Everyone is watching!

INSIGHT

Look at the second sentence. Is the subject *everyone* singular or plural? For a hint, write both parts of the verb here: _____ Is the verb *is watching* used with singular or plural subjects? _____ You're right if you said singular. The helping verb *is* should be your clue. A word like *everyone* is tricky. The meaning seems to be plural, but in fact the word is singular. If you break down the word *everyone*, you can see the word *one*. Of course *one* is singular! Following is a list of some other subjects that are always singular.

Subjects that are always singular			
everyone	everybody	everything	every
anyone	anybody	anything	each
someone	somebody	something	
either (one)	neither (one)		
no one	nobody	nothing	

The word parts *one*, *body*, and *thing* tell you the word is singular. The words *every*, *each*, *either*, and *neither* also are singular.

PRACTICE 1

Choose the correct verb for each sentence. Write it on the line.

1. (*is/are*) Everyone _____ watching.

2. (*is/are*) Don't be silly! Nobody _____ paying any attention.

3. (*seems/seem*) Everything _____ to bother you these days.

4. (*make/makes*) Each little problem _____ you nervous.

5. (*worries/worry*) No one _____ as much as you do.

6. (*is/are*) I think you should see a doctor or take a long vacation. Neither solution _____ cheap, I know.

Answers start on page 174.

Subjects That Are Always Plural

Here is another type of tricky subject. What is wrong with this sentence?

My favorite pants is ripped.

INSIGHT

This may seem OK since only one pair of pants is being talked about, but *pants* is a subject that is *always* plural.

My favorite pants **are** ripped.

Subjects that are always plural	
pants	scissors
trousers	clothes
jeans	glasses (eyeglasses)

Is anything wrong with this sentence?

My favorite pair of pants is caught on a bicycle chain.

No! Why? To find out, locate the subject of the sentence and write it here: _____
If you wrote *pair*, you were right. *Pair* is a singular noun. *Of pants* is just an interrupting phrase that tells more about *pair*. You have already studied such phrases on pages 104–106.

Do not confuse the subject of a sentence with part of an interrupting phrase.

PRACTICE 2

Underline the subject of each sentence. Then choose the correct verb. Write it on the line. The first one has been done for you.

1. (*is/are*) My favorite <u>pair</u> of pants **is** caught in a bicycle chain.

2. (*is cutting/are cutting*) These scissors _____ you free.

3. (*is/are*) Don't do that! These trousers _____ my best pair!

4. (*belongs/belong*) That old pair of jeans _____ in the trash.

5. (*makes/make*) Your dirty pair of glasses _____ everything look bad.

6. (*was/were*) My clothes _____ the best that money can buy.

Answers start on page 174.

Noncount Nouns as Subjects

These doughnuts **look** good.
This chocolate doughnut **looks** very good.
The coffee **looks** tasty too.

INSIGHT

Review now what you learned on pages 67–69. What kind of noun are the words *doughnut* and *doughnuts*?   **a.** count   **b.** noncount

What kind of noun is the word *coffee*?   **a.** count   **b.** noncount

You're right if you saw that the first two are count nouns; that is, you can say "one doughnut," "two doughnuts," etc. You're right if you said *coffee* was a noncount noun because you can't count one coffee, two coffees, and so on. (You can say "one *cup* of coffee," "two *cups* of coffee," etc.) Does the verb form in the third sentence go with a singular or plural subject? _____

Noncount subjects use the same verb forms as singular subjects.

PRACTICE 3

Choose the correct verb and write it on the line.

1. (*looks/look*) The coffee _____ tasty.

2. (*is/are*) My cream _____ spoiled.

3. (*is/are*) My cookies _____ delicious.

4. (*gets/get*) Cereal _____ soggy if you don't eat it right away.

5. (*has/have*) This meal _____ its good and bad points.

6. (*makes/make*) Hunger _____ me eat everything in sight.

Answers start on page 174.

PROOFREAD

Find and correct the errors with verb forms. Check the subject-verb agreement. Cross out the wrong word and write the correct word above it. There are eight mistakes in all, and the first one has been corrected for you.

Problems with money ~~is~~ *are* major troubles in someone's life. If someone don't have enough money, he or she cannot pay for food, rent, clothing, and other things. Good, cheap food become hard to find. Clothes gets torn and shabby looking.

The solution to money problems are to find a good job. However, not everyone are able to do this. People without work has to depend on the government for support. No one get rich on government money.

Answers start on page 174.

HERE/THERE

Here's Johnny!

Here is the table.
There is a bottle on the table.
There go the guests.

INSIGHT

What are the subjects of these sentences? Before you answer, here is an important rule:
Here and *there* are not nouns or pronouns and cannot be subjects of sentences. Now,
what is the subject of each sentence? _____ , _____ , and _____ .
You're right if you wrote *table, bottle,* and *guests.* Finding the subject of a sentence
that begins with *here* or *there* can be tricky because the subject comes *after* the verb.
To help find the subject, try turning the sentence around in your mind:

The table is here.
A bottle is on the table there.
The guests go there.

> **The words *there* and *here* are never subjects of sentences.**
> **To find the subject of a sentence beginning with *there* or *here*,**
> **switch the order around.**

PRACTICE 1

Underline the subject of each sentence. Then decide if the verb is the correct one for
the subject.

- If it is, write *OK* on the line.
- If it isn't, cross it out and write the correct form above it.

The first two have been done for you.

_____ 1. There ~~are~~ **is** more juice in the
refrigerator.

OK 2. Here comes the bride.

_____ 3. There is glasses right at the
edge of the table.

_____ 4. Here is trouble waiting to
happen.

_____ 5. Here sit the hostess of the party.

_____ 6. There is fun and games still
to come.

_____ 7. There are dip and cheese
still unopened.

_____ 8. There go your wife.

Answers start on page 175.

Common Problems

There ain't no doughnuts on the table.
There ain't no wine left in the bottle.

What is wrong with these two sentences? You've studied this problem already: both use the word *ain't* and both use double negatives! There are two ways to fix these sentences:

WAY 1: There **are no** doughnuts on the table.
There **is no** wine left in the bottle.
WAY 2: There **aren't any** doughnuts on the table.
There **isn't any** wine left in the bottle.

Here is another problem.

WRONG: It is some wine in the bottle.
WRONG: They is some wine in the bottle.
RIGHT: There is some wine in the bottle.

Never use *it* or *they* instead of *there*. What is wrong with this sentence?

There a big cork in that bottle.

This sentence has no verb. Remember, *here* and *there* are not subjects, and they aren't verbs, either. You must write a verb after either of these words.

There **is** a big cork in that bottle.

PRACTICE 2

Look at the picture below. Notice what is there and what *isn't* there.

Complete the sentences below using *There is, There are, There isn't,* or *There aren't* with *a, some,* or *any.* Make sure your sentences agree with what is actually in the picture. The first one has been done for you.

1. **There is a** _____ bottle on the table.

2. _____ wine in the bottle.

3. _____ glasses on the table.

4. _____ wine in the glasses.

5. _____ bag on the table.

6. _____ doughnuts in the bag.

7. _____ taco chips in the bag.

8. _____ onion dip in the container.

9. _____ cheese on the table.

10. _____ ice cream on the table.

PROOFREAD

Find and correct the mistakes. Cross out wrong words and write the correct words above. If a word is missing, draw an arrow and write the word. There are eight mistakes in all, and the first one has been corrected for you.

> In my kitchen, ~~it~~ **there** is only one cabinet. There is a lot of food in it. There
>
> is two jars of jelly. There is four cans of soup. They is a box of cereal.
>
> There are five bottles of salad dressing. There some spices, too, but there
>
> ain't no sugar. There isn't no salt, either. I have to buy a pound of sugar
>
> and a pound of salt.

Answers start on page 175.

CUMULATIVE REVIEW

Show What You Know

Last month, there was a costume party. Look at the picture to see what was happening at midnight.

WRITING ASSIGNMENT

Write eight sentences about the party. Describe the scene and tell what everyone was doing. Use the past continuous (*Everyone was dancing the jitterbug*) or the verb *be* (*No one was unhappy*). Use the following phrases to begin your sentences. The first one has been completed for you.

1. Last month there was a costume party. The guests at midnight __were__ __still enjoying themselves.__

2. The man in the gorilla costume _____.

3. The woman wearing the witch outfit _____.

4. The man in the karate suit _____.

5. The people in the horse costume _____.

6. The drinks and the food _____.

7. The fun _____.

8. No one _____.

9. Everyone _____.

Answers will vary.

CHAPTER 8
WRITING CORRECT AND COMPLETE SENTENCES

Goals

- To avoid writing sentence fragments and run-on sentences
- To use transition words
- To join two simple sentences together
- To write sentences with two or more verbs
- To connect a series of three or more items with commas
- To know when *not* to use a comma

AVOIDING FRAGMENTS

Something Is Missing

A smoke bomb.

INSIGHT

Look at the words above. Do you see a complete sentence? _____ You may remember from the beginning of the book that a sentence must tell a complete idea. The words above do not tell a complete idea. You might ask, "What about the smoke bomb? Did someone buy it? Did it explode? Did someone throw it on the baseball field?" Without more information in the sentence, you will probably feel confused.

What exactly is needed to make those words into a sentence? For one thing, we need a verb—like *buy, throw*, or *explode*. Every sentence needs a verb, so the words can become a sentence if a verb is added, like this:

A smoke bomb **exploded**.

What is the verb? _____ What is the subject? _____ The verb is *exploded*, and the subject is *smoke bomb*.

115

Look at another example. Is this a sentence?

Threw a smoke bomb on the field.

This is not a sentence. Let's see why not. It is true that there is a verb—*threw*. There is also an object—*smoke bomb*—so you know what was thrown. But *who* threw the smoke bomb? There is no subject! Remember that a subject tells who or what does the action of the verb. Let's add a subject to get a complete sentence:

A man threw a smoke bomb on the field.

Both of these are now two good sentences: *A smoke bomb exploded* and *A man threw a smoke bomb on the field*. Both sentences have a subject and a verb.

> **A sentence tells a complete idea.**
> **A sentence must have a subject and a verb.**

We looked at two groups of words that were not sentences: *A smoke bomb* and *Threw a smoke bomb*. These are called **fragments** because they are not complete sentences. They are missing a verb or a subject.

> **A fragment is missing a subject or a verb.**
> **Write complete sentences, not fragments.**

PRACTICE 1

All of the following are good sentences. Underline each subject and verb and write *S* and *V*. The first one has been done for you.

1. A smoke bomb exploded.

2. A man with a beer can threw it.

3. He was drunk.

4. His team was losing.

5. The police arrested the drunk man.

PRACTICE 2

All of the following are fragments. There are no sentences. Write what each is missing: a subject or a verb. The first one has been done for you.

1. The pitcher of the team.   (What's missing? **verb**)

2. Caught the ball.   (What's missing? _____)

3. Jumped high in the air.   (What's missing? _____)

4. The angry fans.   (What's missing? _____)

5. The player in left field.   (What's missing? _____)

PRACTICE 3

Read each group of words. Is it a sentence or a fragment? If a subject or verb is missing, you know you have a fragment.

- Circle SENT. for sentence or FRAG. for fragment.
- If you circle FRAG., tell what is missing—the subject or verb.

The first two have been done for you.

SENT.   (FRAG.)   **1.** Threw a smoke bomb on the field.

(What's missing? **subject**)

(SENT.)   FRAG.   **2.** Someone threw a smoke bomb.

(What's missing? _____)

SENT.   FRAG.   **3.** The team was losing.

(What's missing? _____)

SENT.   FRAG.   **4.** The people in the bleachers.

(What's missing? _____)

SENT.   FRAG.   **5.** Shouted at the players.

(What's missing? _____)

SENT.   FRAG.   **6.** The batter on the other team hit a home run.

(What's missing? _____)

SENT.   FRAG.   **7.** Lost the last game of the season.

(What's missing? _____)

SENT.   FRAG.   **8.** The silent fans slowly left the ballpark.

(What's missing? _____)

SENT.   FRAG.   **9.** Talked about all their mistakes.

(What's missing? _____)

SENT.   FRAG.   **10.** The unhappy players in the showers.

(What's missing? _____)

Answers start on page 175.

Fixing Fragments

Many students write fragments when they mean to write sentences. Let's work on how to fix fragments.

What's missing from this fragment?

Hit the ball to left field.

You're right if you noticed that the subject is missing. To make the fragment into a sentence, add a subject. Write your own example on the line.

_____ hit the ball to left field.

What's missing from the next fragment?

>   The excited fans.

You're right if you saw that the verb is missing. What did the fans *do*? Maybe they screamed. Write the verb *screamed* on the line to complete the sentence.

>   The excited fans _____.

Now you have a complete sentence. It is fine as it is, but you could make it longer by adding more information if you want to. You could add an adverb to it like *loudly*, *wildly*, or *crazily*. You could also add a place like *from the bleachers* or *in the stands*. Then you would end up with sentences like these:

>   The excited fans screamed.
>   The excited fans screamed wildly from the bleachers.

Both of these are complete sentences even though one is short and one is long. Each one has a subject and a verb and tells a complete idea.

PRACTICE 4

Correct each fragment below. Rewrite it, adding a subject or verb and other words as necessary in place of the arrow (∧). There is more than one correct way to fix these fragments. The first one has been done for you.

1. ∧ Went to the baseball game.
   <u>My children and I went to the baseball game.</u>

2. ∧ Ate lots of hot dogs and potato chips.

3. The man next to me ∧.

4. With bases loaded and nobody out, the pitcher ∧.

5. ∧ booed loudly.

6. In fact, some of the fans ∧.

7. The tired children ∧.

8. Finally, ∧ left the game early.

Answers will vary.

Fixing Fragments in a Paragraph

It's easy to fix fragments when they are all alone. It's harder to fix them when they are hiding in a paragraph. See if you can spot the fragments in this paragraph. Look for three fragments and underline them when you find them.

>   Football is a confusing sport. A lot of men in strange uniforms. Violently knock each other down. The action may stop at any minute, though. A man in a black and white shirt. He makes a mysterious hand signal. Suddenly, the players come to a halt. I don't get it!

Check to see that you found the three fragments:

1. A lot of men in strange uniforms.

2. Violently knock each other down.

3. A man in a black and white shirt.

If the ideas are related, you can fix fragments by putting two of them together.

> FRAGMENT 1: A lot of men in strange uniforms. (no verb)
> **+** FRAGMENT 2: Violently knock each other down. (no subject)
>
> SENTENCE: A lot of men in strange uniforms violently knock each other down.

Look back at the sentence and label the subject and the verb with *S* and *V*. Now go on to the next fragment.

Fragment 3 has a subject (*man*) but no verb. You can connect this fragment to the sentence after it, but what happens if you just put the two together as they are?

> A man in a black and white shirt he makes a mysterious hand signal.

This sentence has a double subject—*man* and *he*. The best way to fix this problem is simply to drop *he*:

> A man in a black and white shirt makes a mysterious hand signal.

Look back at the sentence and label the subject and the verb with *S* and *V*.

> **Sometimes fragments can be corrected by joining them to other fragments or sentences.**

PROOFREAD

Find and fix the five fragments. Rewrite the paragraph with your corrections.

> Families often fight. Over the television. The father likes football. The mother of the family. She likes professional golf. The little children like cartoons. Everybody argues. The winner of the argument. Watches his favorite show. The losers of the argument. They must do something else.

Answers start on page 175.

USING TRANSITION WORDS

Meanwhile, Back at the Ranch

Ginny is a seamstress in a dry cleaner's. She begins work at 7:00. **First**, she looks at all of the jobs for the morning. **For example**, she may see several dresses, a pair of pants, and a shirt waiting for her. **Then** she takes a short lunch break. **After lunch**, she concentrates mostly on jobs that were dropped off in the morning. **Occasionally**, she talks to customers. **Finally**, Ginny goes home at 4:00.

INSIGHT

Read the paragraph. Then circle the **boldface** words. Words and phrases like these are called *transitions*. They help the reader move smoothly from sentence to sentence. (Try reading the paragraph out loud *without* the transitions. Without them, it sounds choppy.) Transitions usually go at the beginning of the sentence. A *comma* $\boxed{,}$ is used after most transitions. (There is one exception to learn. Do not use a comma after the word *then*.) After a transition, be sure to write a complete sentence, including a subject and verb.

> **Write a complete sentence after a transition.**
> **You should usually put a comma after a transition.**
> **EXCEPTION: Do not use a comma after the word *then*.**

Here is a list of some common transitions:

First,	Second,	Third,	Finally,
Next,	Then	Later,	Also,
For example,	For instance,	Meanwhile,	In addition,

PRACTICE

Rewrite the paragraph, adding transitions at the arrows (∧) . Make sure your transitions make sense and fit the meaning of the sentences they are used in. Remember to use a capital letter only at the beginning of each sentence or proper noun.

Larry is a shoe salesman. He arrives at work at 9:00. ∧ He talks to his boss. ∧ He works on the shoe displays. ∧ He might put a new set of shoes in the window. He opens the doors at 10:00. ∧ He helps the customers all day long. Larry locks the doors at 6:00. ∧ He helps the boss clean up.

Answers start on page 175.

CUMULATIVE REVIEW

Show What You Know

Remember what you have learned about correcting fragments and using transitions.

PROOFREAD

Find and correct the fragments in this paragraph. You may need to add subjects and verbs to fix the fragments. You may need to join a fragment to a sentence. There are seven fragments in all, and the first two have been corrected for you.

I'd like to tell you about our neighborhood. ~~Have~~ [We have] many service busi-

nesses ~~In~~ [in] this area. For example, you will find dry cleaners, shoe repairs,

and laundromats. In addition, have many retail stores. For instance, shoe

stores, dress shops, and supermarkets. Can also find a few factories. Two

clothing factories and a pizza factory. Our neighborhood. It is good for

business.

Answers start on page 175.

WRITING ASSIGNMENT

Choose *one* of the following topics.

1. Think of a friend or relative with an interesting job. Write a paragraph of about eight sentences about a typical day for this person. Use transition words (*First, Also, etc.*). Remember to use the simple present tense correctly. (*My uncle works for the post office. . . .*)

2. Remember what you did last Saturday (or on your last day off). Write a paragraph of about eight sentences about everything you did from morning until night. Be sure to use transition words and to use the simple past tense correctly. (*I slept until noon. . . .*)

Read over your paragraph and check for the following things:

☑ All your sentences are complete, and there are no fragments.
☑ Verbs agree with subjects.
☑ Transition words are used correctly.

WRITING COMPOUND SENTENCES

Compounding the Interest

1. The river flooded the town. Many people lost their homes.
2. The river flooded the town, and many people lost their homes.

INSIGHT

In line 1, there are two sentences. Go back and underline the subject and verb of each sentence. Then label each with *S* or *V*. Check your answers. In the first sentence, the subject is *river*; the verb is *flooded*. In the second sentence on line 1, the subject is *people*; the verb is *lost*. Now look at how both sentences come together in line 2. What word is used to join the two sentences? _____ What punctuation mark do you see before that word? _____ You're right if you saw that the word *and* after a comma [,] joins the two sentences. *And* is a type of word called a **conjunction**, or joining word.

When you put together two complete sentences with a comma and a conjunction like *and*, you have a **compound sentence**.

**In a compound sentence, two complete sentences are joined together with a comma [,] and a conjunction (like *and*).
There are two subject-verb (S-V) pairs in a compound sentence.**

PRACTICE 1

Join the pairs of sentences with a comma [,] and the word *and*. (Note: Use a small letter, not a capital letter, after *and* unless the word is a proper noun.) The first one has been done for you.

1. It rained for three days. The river flooded.

   It rained for three days, and the river flooded.

2. Water filled the streets. People used boats instead of cars.

3. Parents left their jobs. Children left their schools.

4. Some people stayed with friends. Others went to shelters.

5. The army came to help. The National Guard joined in.

6. Mr. Brown lost his store. Mrs. Jones lost her house.

7. The people rebuilt the town. The government helped.

Answers start on page 175.

PRACTICE 2

Show what you know about different occupations, and practice compound sentences at the same time. Complete each sentence as you wish. Then combine the two sentences to make a compound. The first one has been done for you.

1. Bosses give . . .
   Workers follow . . .

   Bosses give orders. Workers follow them.

   Bosses give orders, and workers follow them.

2. Chefs cook . . .
   Waiters serve . . .

3. Artists paint . . .
   Photographers take . . .

4. Bosses write . . .
   Secretaries type . . .

5. Pilots fly . . .
   Astronauts fly . . .

6. Architects design . . .
   Construction workers build . . .

7. Car salesmen sell . . .
   Customers buy . . .

8. Politicians tell . . .
   Reporters write . . .

Answers will vary.

Combining Sentences with *But*

Cocaine is dangerous, but many people use it.

The sentence above is a compound sentence, but it does not use *and*. You can see a comma before the conjunction. What is the conjunction? _____ You're correct if you wrote *but*. The words *and* and *but* are conjunctions with different meanings. *And* joins two sentences with meanings that go hand in hand. *But* joins two sentences with meanings that show the difference between things or that seem to go against each other.

Look back to the sentence above. The fact that people use cocaine *goes against* the idea that cocaine is dangerous. For this reason, *but* is used as the conjunction.

> ***But* is a conjunction that joins sentences whose meanings show the difference between things or go against each other.**

PRACTICE 3

Combine the following sentences using the word *but*. Remember to put a comma before *but*.

1. Cocaine is dangerous. Many people use it.

2. Cocaine is expensive. Many people buy it.

3. Marijuana is illegal. Many people smoke it.

4. Cigarettes are harmful. Many people smoke them.

5. People read about the dangers. They don't pay attention.

Answers start on page 176.

Combining Sentences with *So*

The baby was crying, so his father picked him up.

The compound sentence above has a new conjunction. What is it? _____ Of course, there is a comma before it. *So* means *for this reason*. It shows the results of something. The baby was crying. For this reason, the father picked him up.

> **So** is a conjunction that means *for this reason.*

PRACTICE 4

Combine these sentences with *so*. Remember to use a comma before *so*.

1. The baby was crying. His father picked him up.

2. The baby was hungry. His mother fed him.

3. He was sick. His father took him to the clinic.

4. He was wet. His mother changed him.

5. He smiled. His mother ran for the camera.

Answers start on page 176.

Review

So far you have studied three conjunctions. Write them here: _____ _____ _____
Each has a different meaning. (Go back and check the definitions if you need to refresh your memory.) Remember that a conjunction after a comma connects two complete sentences. You need two pairs of subjects and verbs.

PRACTICE 5

Read the paragraph below as it stands now. You'll notice that it sounds very choppy. It will sound better if you connect some of the sentences using conjunctions. Rewrite the paragraph, adding commas and *and, but,* or *so* where they are appropriate. The first two sentences have been joined for you.

Bonnie and Jack Randall had a drinking problem ,but they ~~They~~ didn't realize it. Every day Bonnie drank a bottle of wine. Jack drank five martinis. They started to lose all of their friends. They didn't seem to care. One day, Jack showed up at work drunk. His boss fired him. Jack told Bonnie about it. They finally decided to get some help from Alcoholics Anonymous. The Randalls are trying hard to change their lives.

Answers start on page 176.

BECACISE

Because I Said So!

Claudia stayed home because her son was sick.

INSIGHT

Two sentences can be connected with the word *because*. How many subject-verb (S-V) pairs do you see in the sentence above? _____ You're right if you said two:

        S   V   S   V
    Claudia stayed home because her son was sick.

Do you see a comma before the word *because*? _____

> **The word *because* can connect two sentences.**
> **Do not use a comma before *because*.**

PRACTICE 1

Combine the following sentences using *because*. Do not use a comma.

1. Claudia stayed home. Her son was sick.
2. She was worried. He had a high fever.
3. She took him to the clinic. He had a terrible earache.
4. Claudia's boss was upset. She was absent from work.
5. Claudia's husband stayed home the next day. Claudia couldn't miss any more work.

PRACTICE 2

Combine the following sentences using *and*, *but*, *so*, or *because*. Use a comma before any of the first three words. Do not use a comma before *because*. The first two have been done for you.

1. Claudia missed a day of work. Her boss got angry.
   Claudia missed a day of work, and her boss got angry.

2. She returned to work the next day. She was afraid of losing her job.
   She returned to work the next day because she was afraid of losing her job.

3. Rafael stayed with their son. He had the day off.
4. The boy got better. Rafael went back to work the following day.

5. The little boy felt much better. He returned to school.

6. Claudia was relieved. Her son was well again.

7. The little boy recovered completely. Rafael got sick.

8. He went to bed. Claudia called the clinic again.

9. Claudia was exhausted. She didn't get sick.

10. She felt lucky. She stayed well.

Answers start on page 176.

NOTE TO THE INSTRUCTOR:
Grammar Write Away Book 2 helps students distinguish between compound and complex sentences and between independent and dependent clauses. At this level, however, such classifications may be confusing to the student. We include this brief lesson on correctly punctuating complex sentences using *because* in order that students may know how to correctly construct sentences with this commonly used conjunction.

AVOIDING RUN-ONS

Running Off at the Mouth

Many girls drop out of high school they leave to have babies.

INSIGHT

What is wrong with the sentence above? Study it carefully. The problem is this: there are two sentences run together. A sentence like this is called a *run-on*. Run-ons can be confusing and hard to read.

> **Run-ons are two or more sentences run together.**
> **Avoid writing run-ons.**

Look back to the example run-on above. See if you can find where the run-on sentence should be divided. The dividing line should be between the words _____ and _____. To fix a run-on, just add a period and a capital letter in the right place. The correct sentences will look like this:

Many girls drop out of high school.
They leave to have babies.

> **To fix a run-on, put a period and a capital letter in the right place.**

How do you know where to divide a run-on? Try thinking about the ideas, and see if there is a natural break. You can also try reading the run-on out loud and make the break at the place where your voice naturally pauses.

PRACTICE 1

Fix these run-ons. Put a period and a capital letter in the right place. The first one has been done for you.

1. Many teenage girls drop out of school they leave to have babies.

    Many teenage girls drop out of school.
    They leave to have babies.

2. These girls are very young some of them are under fifteen.

3. A teenage mother can lose her freedom she can also lose her education.

4. A teenage mother can finish her education it is difficult, though.

Answers start on page 176.

More Help with Run-ons

Now that you've gotten a basic feel for what run-ons are and how to divide them, here are some basic rules for finding and fixing them.

Look for subjects and verbs. Keep in mind that every sentence has a subject-verb pair (S-V pair). Every compound sentence has two S-V pairs, *but* there is a comma and a conjunction between the pairs. Compare the two correct sentences with the two run-ons below.

First, let's look at the two correct sentences.

CORRECT: Teenagers sometimes drop out. They lose their education.

A period divides these two sentences. Each sentence has a subject-verb (S-V) pair. Now look at another way that these ideas could be connected.

CORRECT: Teenagers sometimes drop out, and they lose their education.

How many subject-verb pairs are in this sentence? _____ You're right if you said two. What word and punctuation mark divide the two parts of the sentence? _____ They are divided by a comma [,] and the word *and*.

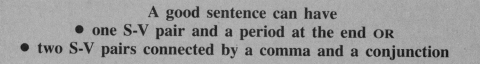

A good sentence can have
- **one S-V pair and a period at the end OR**
- **two S-V pairs connected by a comma and a conjunction**

Now use your understanding of subject-verb pairs to recognize run-on sentences.

RUN-ON: Teenagers sometimes drop out they lose their education.

Why is this a run-on? How many subject-verb pairs do you see? _____ Does anything divide the two parts of the sentence? _____ There are two S-V pairs, but nothing divides them. There is no period, and there is no comma or conjunction.

RUN-ON: Teenagers sometimes drop out, they lose their education.

The two parts of this sentence are separated by a comma, but a comma without a conjunction cannot divide two S-V pairs.

There are two basic ways to correct a run-on:
- **Add a period and a capital letter in the right place.**
- **Add a comma and a conjunction in the right place.**

PRACTICE 2

Find the good sentences and the run-ons.

- First label the subjects *S* and the verbs *V*.
- Circle any periods *or* commas and conjunctions.
- Write *run-on* or *OK*.

The first two have been done for you.

run-on 1. Education is important it can be difficult.

OK 2. Education is important, but it is often hard.

_____ 3. Some people quit school they lose their education.

_____ 4. Sometimes they change their minds, and they go back to school.

_____ 5. Some people return to high school others get their GED.

_____ 6. An education gives you basic skills, it also gives you the chance for a decent job.

_____ 7. A diploma is not a guarantee, but it can help you.

_____ 8. A diploma means hard work. The effort is worth it.

PRACTICE 3

Look for run-ons in the paragraph. Correct them by adding a period and a capital letter in the right place. You may need to change a comma to a period. (If a sentence is a good sentence, do not change anything.) There are four mistakes in all, and the first one has been corrected for you.

Young people drop out of high school for different reasons. One reason
is problems in the school. Some schools are dangerous they are full of
gangs. Serious students are often afraid to come to school, and they quit.
In addition, some young women get pregnant, they soon leave to give birth
to their babies the babies need care, so the mothers don't want to leave them.

PRACTICE 4

Fix these run-ons by adding the conjunctions *and, but*, or *so*. Read the sentences carefully to choose the word that best fits the meaning. Remember to put a comma before these words.

1. Karen was seventeen years old she was nine months pregnant.

2. She wanted her baby she also wanted her education.

3. She wanted to stay in school she had to leave.

4. Karen had a baby boy she loved him very much.

5. She didn't have enough money she couldn't give him many toys or clothes.

6. She wanted a job she couldn't find one.

7. She wanted to go back to school she didn't want to leave her baby alone.

8. She wanted to give her son plenty of opportunities she wanted to further her own education.

PROOFREAD

Read some more about Karen. Check the paragraph for run-ons. You can fix each run-on in one of three ways:

- Add periods and capital letters.
- Add a comma and *and, but*, or *so*.
- Add *because*.

Make sure your corrected sentences make sense! There are seven run-ons in all, and the first has been corrected for you.

    Karen talked to a friend in her neighborhood. ~~her~~ **Her** friend told her about a special school program for teenage mothers. The school has a day-care center right in the building the young mothers can bring their children to school. The children are cared for, the mothers can study at the same time. Karen joined the program, she is very pleased with it. She brings her son to the day-care center in room 101 then she goes to room 202 for her classes. Karen is taking a class in child care she wants to learn how to be a better mother. She also works with a program for other teenagers in the high school, in this program she tells them to wait before having a baby.

Answers start on page 176.

NOTE TO THE INSTRUCTOR:
Students may also want to use other subordinating conjunctions like *when, where, who,* or *while,* to combine the sentences. If this is the case, point out to the student that no comma is needed before these words.

REVIEW

Fragments and Run-ons

Remember that a _____ is a sentence that is not complete. A _____ is two sentences run together. (You should have written *fragment* first and then *run-on*.)

Review what you have learned about good sentences and about fragments and run-ons.

PRACTICE 1

Look at each sentence. Is it a good sentence, a fragment, or a run-on? Mark the subjects and verbs with *S* and *V*, and circle the commas and conjunctions. Write *OK*, *frag*, or *run-on*. The first two have been done for you.

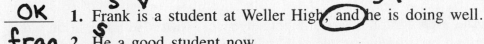

OK   1. Frank is a student at Weller High, and he is doing well.

frag   2. He a good student now.

_____   3. Gets good grades in school.

_____   4. He studies hard he is also active in sports.

_____   5. He plays on the school soccer team.

_____   6. This year he is happy last year he wasn't.

_____   7. Last year had a problem with drugs.

_____   8. His friends were using crack he wanted it too.

_____   9. Didn't want to seem different.

_____   10. His grades went down, and he stopped attending school.

_____   11. Then a school counselor talked to Frank.

_____   12. Convinced Frank to join an anti-drug program.

_____   13. Was hard, but Frank gave up the drugs.

_____   14. Frank is repeating tenth grade, this time he is doing well.

_____   15. Frank a lucky young man.

Answers start on page 177.

PRACTICE 2

Check your answers to Practice 1. Then think of ways to fix all of the run-ons and fragments in that exercise. Put your corrected sentences together to make a paragraph. Write the paragraph on a separate piece of paper.

Answers will vary.

CUMULATIVE REVIEW

Show What You Know

It is easy to write run-ons and fragments by mistake. Even experienced writers make these mistakes. For this reason, you should always check for run-ons and fragments after you write something, whether it's a few sentences, a paragraph, or a full essay. There are two ways to do this:

- Check each sentence to make sure it has a subject and a verb. Make sure that a sentence with two or more S-V pairs has a conjunction like *and, but, so*, or *because*.
- Read (or whisper) your paragraph out loud. Stop only when you reach a period, and pause only where you have written a comma. This will often help you *hear* any run-ons or fragments.

Now get ready to write a paragraph of about eight sentences. In it, use a transition word every time you mention a different problem. Use transition words like *First, Second, Also,* and *Finally.*

WRITING ASSIGNMENT

Choose *one* of these topics:

1. What are some of the problems in the high schools of this country? Think about the students, the teachers, the classes, and the buildings and grounds. Be specific.

2. What are or were some of the problems in *your* school? (You can talk about elementary school, junior high, or high school.) Think about the students, the teachers, the classes, and the building and grounds. Be specific.

Read over your paragraph and check for the following things:

☑ Verbs agree with subjects.
☑ Transition words are used correctly.
☑ There are no fragments and run-ons.

COMPOUND VERBS

Eat, Drink, and Be Merry

1. The audience clapped. The audience whistled.
2. The audience clapped and whistled.

INSIGHT

In the first line, there are two sentences. The subject of each sentence is the same: _____. The verbs are different: _____ and _____. In the second line, the two sentences have been combined into one. The subject is still *audience*, and the two verbs are joined with the word _____.

Go back to the second line and write *S* over the subject and *V* over the first and second verbs. Note that the subject goes with both *clapped* and *whistled*. There is one subject but more than one verb. In other words, the sentence in the second line has a *compound verb*. Do you see a comma before *and*? _____

> **Two verbs in a sentence can be joined with the word *and*.**
> **Do not use a comma before *and* in this situation.**

You do not use a comma because you are not joining two complete sentences.

PRACTICE 1

Combine the two sentences into one sentence with *and* and a compound verb. The first one has been done for you.

1. The audience clapped. The audience whistled.

   <u>The audience clapped and whistled.</u>

2. The band bowed. The band played another song.

3. The lead singer sang. The lead singer shouted.

4. The back-up singers sang. The back-up singers danced.

5. The guitarists played. The guitarists jumped up in the air.

6. The drummer beat out a rhythm. The drummer played a solo.

7. The people sang along. The people danced in the aisles.

Answers start on page 177.

Three or More Verbs

The audience clapped enthusiastically, whistled loudly, and
shouted for more.

In the sentence above, find the subject and label it with *S*. (You should have marked *audience*.) Now look for the verbs. How many do you see? _____ Label the three verbs with *V*. Finally, look for the commas. Circle each one. (You should have circled two commas.)

> **Three or more verbs can be joined in a sentence.**
> **Use the word *and* before the last verb.**
> **Use a comma after each verb that comes before *and*.**

In this case, you use a comma even though you are not joining complete sentences. You use commas when you join three or more verbs (or nouns, adjectives, or adverbs).

PRACTICE 2

Combine the three or more sentences using commas and the word *and*. The first one has been done for you.

1. The audience clapped enthusiastically. The audience whistled loudly. The audience shouted.

   <u>The audience clapped enthusiastically, whistled loudly, and shouted.</u>

2. The band smiled. The band bowed. The band left the stage.

3. We put on our coats. We picked up our bags. We left the concert hall.

4. We got in the car. We drove to a restaurant. We ordered a pizza.

5. We ate two pizzas. We drank two pitchers of cola. We talked for three hours.

6. I went home. I put on my pajamas. I fell asleep right away.

Answers start on page 177.

Agreement with Two or More Verbs

Maria sings and plays the piano.

In the sentence above, the subject is *Maria*. Look at the verbs *sings* and *plays*. Each verb ends in the letter ____. Notice that each verb agrees with the subject.

> **In a sentence with a compound verb,**
> **each verb should agree with the subject.**

PRACTICE 3

Read each sentence and correct the error in the verb form. The first one has been done for you.

1. Maria sings and ~~play~~ *plays* the piano.

2. She often writes and perform her own music.

3. She thinks up the melody, tries it out, and write it down.

4. Maria's parents love their daughter and respects her talent.

5. They read her songs, listen to her music, and is very proud of her.

6. Maria sing well and hopes for a successful future in music.

Answers start on page 177.

Common Problems

> The baby was screaming and cry.

Something is wrong with the sentence above. Look at the verbs. Which verb is wrong? Write it here: _____ Did you write *cry*? If so, you're right. The verb *cry* should end in *ing* just like the first verb, *screaming*. That is because both verbs go with the same subject and the same helping verb. The subject is *baby* and the helping verb is _____. Think of the sentence like this:

> The baby was screaming and crying.

Try another problem sentence:

> The father held him and rocking him.

Now which verb is wrong? _____ You're right if you said *rocking*. The correct form would be *rocked*—the simple past tense. Both verbs, *held* and *rocked*, go with the same subject: the _____. There is no helping verb, so the *ing* form is incorrect. Here is the correct sentence:

> The father **held** him and **rocked** him.

**When two or more verbs are combined by the word *and*,
make sure all the forms are the same.**

PRACTICE 4

Rewrite each sentence correctly. Fix either the first or second verb so that both forms are the same and are correct. The first one has been done for you.

1. The baby was screaming and cry.

   The baby was screaming and crying.

2. The father picked him up and offering him a bottle.

3. His baby drink the milk and smiled happily.

4. Babies often scream and cried.

5. They want to eat and getting attention.

6. A comfortable baby will shut its eyes and falling asleep.

7. Parents know and responds to their baby's needs.

8. Does a good parent always know and responding correctly?

9. Even a good parent will misunderstand and making a mistake sometimes.

10. When you were a child, your parents feed you and gave you attention.

11. You needed food and also want love.

Answers start on page 178.

PRACTICE 5

Now you complete the sentences by adding the word *and*, another verb, and anything else you need to complete the sentence. Be sure that the verb you add matches the form of the verb before *and*. The first one has been done for you.

1. I like to eat . . . and . . .

   I like to eat nachos and drink orange juice.

2. I like to eat . . . and . . .

3. I like to listen . . . and . . .

4. As a child, I went . . . and . . .

5. As a child, I rode . . . and . . .

6. Now I live . . . and . . .

7. I read . . . and . . .

8. Right now I am studying . . . and . . .

9. I want to buy . . . and . . .

10. In the future, I am going to finish my education . . . and . . .

Answers will vary.

CUMULATIVE REVIEW

Show What You Know

Have you ever tried writing a story? In this assignment, you'll get a chance to write a paragraph telling the story that is taking place in a series of pictures. You'll also get a chance to experiment with compound sentences, compound subjects and verbs, and transition words.

- First, before you write the actual story, *plan* what you're going to say. Write down some sentences about the most important things that are happening in the pictures.
- Check to make sure that you have written down events in the order in which they are shown.
- You can write your paragraph in either the present or the past tense, but check over your sentences to make sure you have not switched back and forth between the two tenses.
- Now write your story, putting together the ideas from your plan. Try to combine some of the subjects or verbs, or try to combine sentences using *and, but, so,* or *because.* Use transitions to show shifts in the action.

Here is an example of a plan and the story that came from it. Notice how the writer combined sentences and used transitions to make the writing smoother.

Plan:

1. Two college boys went to a nightclub.
2. They watched a very beautiful singer.
3. One of the boys went backstage.
4. He talked to her.
5. The singer turned into a vampire.
6. The singer bit the boy.
7. He turned into a vampire, too.
8. He tried to bite his friend.
9. The singer tried to bite his friend.
10. They chased him around.
11. The boy found some gasoline.
12. The boy found some rags.
13. He started a fire.
14. The nightclub burned down.
15. The boy ran away.

Story:

Two college boys went to a nightclub, **and** they watched a very beautiful singer. One of the boys went backstage **and** talked to her. **Suddenly,** the singer turned into a vampire **and** bit the boy. **Then** he turned into a vampire, too. He **and the singer** tried to bite his friend. They chased him around. The boy found some gasoline **and some rags, and** he started a fire. **Finally,** the nightclub burned down, **and** the boy ran away.

WRITING ASSIGNMENT

Now it's your turn. Write a plan, then a paragraph of about eight sentences, based on the pictures below. When you are finished writing, check over your paragraph:

☑ There are no fragments and run-ons.
☑ Transition words are used correctly.
☑ You have used a comma and the words *and, but, so,* or *because* to put two sentences together.
☑ Compound verbs are in the same form.
☑ Verbs agree with subjects.

USING COMMAS

Joanna, Zack, and Bill

You have worked on joining two sentences together by adding a comma and a conjunction. You've also worked on joining three or more verbs with commas. Now you'll learn more ways to use a comma.

Bill loved, worshipped, and respected Joanna.
He called her in the morning, in the afternoon, and at night.
Zack was handsome, rich, and elegant.
He gave Joanna flowers, furs, and jewelry.
Bill, Zack, and Joanna had a problem.

INSIGHT

Notice that each sentence includes a series of words or phrases.

● Circle all the commas in the sentences above.
● Circle the word *and* in each sentence.
● Then underline the three items connected by commas or the word *and*. The first one is already done.

The first sentence is like the sentences you have already studied. Here, three verbs are joined with commas and the word *and*. In the next four sentences, you see other items joined by commas and the word *and*.

> **In a series of three or more items (words or phrases),**
> **use the word *and* before the last item.**
> **Use a comma after each item before the word *and*.**

PRACTICE 1

Write your own sentences using these words. Use commas correctly. The first one has been done for you.

1. crunchy—sweet—delicious

The candy was crunchy, sweet, and delicious.

2. ate—drank—danced
3. Andre—Shawn—Winona
4. tall—dark—handsome
5. quickly—silently—carefully

6. intelligent—kind—beautiful
7. ice cream—cookies—chocolate cake
8. in the library—in the cafeteria—at home
9. peace—freedom—brotherhood

Answers will vary.

A Common Problem

Remember that commas are used only when joining *three or more* items. No comma is used when only two items are joined.

> CORRECT: Zack was handsome, rich, and elegant.
> CORRECT: Zack was handsome and rich.
> INCORRECT: Zack was handsome, and rich.

Do not use a comma when joining only two items.

PRACTICE 2

Look at the following groups of sentences. Write a new sentence for each group by joining the words or phrases in **boldface** with *and*. Use commas only where necessary. The first two have been done for you.

1. **Zack** wanted to marry Joanna. **Bill** wanted to marry Joanna.
   Zack and Bill wanted to marry Joanna.

2. Zack was **handsome**. Zack was **rich**. Zack was **elegant**.
   Zack was handsome, rich, and elegant.

3. Bill was **intelligent**. Bill was **kind**.

4. Zack gave Joanna **diamonds**. Zack gave Joanna **rubies**. Zack gave Joanna **emeralds**.

5. Bill sent Joanna **small pictures**. Bill sent Joanna **love letters**.

6. Joanna wanted **money**. Joanna wanted **respect**. Joanna wanted **love**.

7. Bill **loved** her. Bill **helped** her. Bill **talked to** her.

8. Bill **helped Joanna with her career**. Bill **talked to her about her problems**. Bill **promised eternal love**.

9. Zack offered **money**. Zack offered **prestige**.

10. After their wedding, **Joanna** argued all the time. After their wedding, **Zack** argued all the time.

11. Joanna **thought for a long time**. Joanna **made up her mind**.

12. Joanna **gave up Zack**. Joanna **married Bill**.

Answers start on page 178.

Review

You have studied different ways to use commas. Review them now. Read the following sentences:

1. Joanna was in love with Bill, but then she met Zack.
2. Zack bought Joanna gifts, took her to nice restaurants, and gave her many compliments.

Sentence 1 is a compound sentence. That is, two complete sentences are combined using a comma and a conjunction. There are two S-V pairs. In sentence 2, three items are connected by commas and the word *and*.

- Use a comma in a compound sentence (with two S-V pairs) before a conjunction like *and, but,* or *so.*
  EXAMPLE: Joanna liked adventure, and she loved excitement.
- Use commas in a series of three or more items in a sentence. A comma goes after each item before the word *and.*
  EXAMPLE: Her hobbies included playing piano in a bar, mountain climbing, and motorcycle riding.

PROOFREAD

In the short paragraph, put commas where they are needed. There are thirteen commas needed, and the first one has been put in for you.

Joanna wanted love, but she also wanted money. A rich man proposed to her and she thought she'd find happiness with him. He promised her fast cars fine wine and fancy clothes. He delivered his promises but he didn't make Joanna happy. The gifts were exciting but the man wasn't. The rich man was quiet boring and unadventurous. He had wanted her to stay home so she had quit her job. Joanna became lonely bored and frustrated. The expensive clothes the beautiful house and the elegant furniture were not enough for Joanna.

Answers start on page 178.

A Note About Transitions

On page 120, you learned that commas frequently follow transition words. This is not a hard and fast rule, but you will generally be safe if you put a comma after transitions like *First, Next, After that,* and *Finally.* Some other transitions usually followed by a comma are the following: *In addition, Moreover, Furthermore, However,* and *As a result.*

EXAMPLES: First, Joanna told Bill he was too poor.
In addition, she told him she didn't want to date him anymore.
However, Bill hoped Joanna would change her mind.

PARALLEL STRUCTURE

Thinking, Writing, and Fixing

1. Bill's business made signs for stores, businesses, and billboards.
2. At her job, Joanna set up displays of new records, tapes, and showed compact discs.

INSIGHT

One of these sentences is incorrect. To find out which one, look at the items separated by the commas. Write the three items in sentence 1 here: _____, _____, _____. *Stores, businesses,* and *billboards* are all **a.** nouns   **b.** verbs You're right if you said they are all nouns.

Now, what are the three items separated by commas in sentence 2? _____, _____, _____.

Records and *tapes* are both **a.** nouns   **b.** verbs. *Showed* is a **a.** noun   **b.** verb.

You're right if you saw that the first two are nouns but the last item is a verb. Sentence 2 is the one that's incorrect. The items in a series should all be *parallel;* that is, they should all be the same type of word.

> At her job, Joanna set up displays of new records, tapes, and **compact discs.**

Here is another example of a sentence whose items aren't parallel:

> Bill's hobbies were playing saxophone, shooting baskets, and to skydive.

Here, all the verbs should end in *ing*.

> Bill's hobbies were playing saxophone, shooting baskets, and **skydiving.**

> **With a series of two or more items, be sure that the items are the same type of word or are in the same form.**

PRACTICE 1

Some of the sentences below have parallel structure, but others are incorrect. Write *OK* on the line if the sentence is correct. Circle the item that is incorrect if the items in the sentence are not parallel. The first two have been done for you.

__OK__ 1. Bill's life outside of work was interesting and exciting.

_____ 2. Bill's hobbies were playing saxophone, shooting baskets, and (to skydive.)

_____ 3. Bill was good at passing, dribbling, and to get rebounds.

_____ **4.** Skydiving is expensive, fun, and somewhat dangerous.

_____ **5.** Bill's job was routine, dull, and had few events.

_____ **6.** However, he got good pay, plenty of vacation, and took a few personal days.

_____ **7.** Bill enjoyed traveling, meeting people, and adventurous.

_____ **8.** His life was interesting and rewards.

PRACTICE 2

All of these sentences are not parallel. Rewrite the sentence to make it parallel. The first one has been done for you.

1. At her job, Joanna set up displays of new records, tapes, and showed compact discs.

   At her job, Joanna set up displays of new records, tapes, and compact discs.

2. Joanna managed the staff and working noon to eight P.M.

3. She also liked hobbies that were adventurous, active, and to have fun.

4. She enjoyed playing the piano, mountain climbing, and took photographs.

5. She used her savings to buy a motorcycle and taking a trip around the country.

6. She always rode carefully and to show caution.

7. Money can't guarantee adventure, fun, and exciting.

Answers start on page 178.

WHEN NOT TO USE A COMMA

Overdoing It

You have learned when to use a comma. Sometimes people are so worried about using commas correctly that they use them even when they shouldn't. Make sure to use a comma only when you know there is a reason to do so. The following shows the cases where people often put in unnecessary commas. Count the number of combined items in each sentence below. Then try to find the comma mistakes.

Bill was intelligent, and interesting.
Bill worked hard, and did exciting things.
Bill gave Joanna small pictures, and other keepsakes.

INSIGHT

What is the comma mistake? Each sentence lists only two items, so no commas are needed. Cross them out in the sentences above.

> **No comma is needed if only *two* items are combined with *and*.**

Now look for a different kind of comma problem.

The rich man, didn't please Joanna.
Joanna, got frustrated with her life.
A man with a lot of money, is not always the best choice.

First, label the subject and verb of each sentence with *S* and *V*. Where are the commas in each sentence? You're right if you said they are between the subject and the verb. Cross them out. They do not belong.

> **No comma is needed between a subject and a verb.**

Here is another comma problem. Cross out the comma that does not belong.

Joanna married Zack, because he had a lot of money.

> **No comma is needed before the word *because*.**

PRACTICE 1

Some of these sentences use commas correctly, but others use them incorrectly. Cross out the commas that don't belong. Remember the rules for using commas. The first one has been done for you.

1. Joanna ✗ was married to Zack for five years.

2. She worked on the marriage, but Zack made no effort.

3. The marriage of her dreams, turned into a prison.

4. She wanted her own career, and a happy life.

5. She finally left Zack, because she was miserable.

6. She was no longer rich, so she went back to work.

7. Her new job was interesting, and challenging.

8. Joanna saved her money, rented a nice apartment, and bought some new furniture.

9. She picked up the phone, and called Bill.

Answers start on page 178.

A Serious Comma Mistake

You've learned about three common comma mistakes. Now look at an example of another very common kind of comma problem:

> Bill answered the phone after five rings, he was very surprised to hear Joanna's voice.

The writer has strung two sentences together using a comma. The result is a run-on sentence! As you recall, one way to fix a run-on is to add a period and a capital letter to make the run-on two separate sentences.

> Bill answered the phone after five rings. **He** was very surprised to hear Joanna's voice.

You can also fix this comma mistake by adding a conjunction after the comma. Make sure the conjunction fits the meaning of the sentence.

> Bill answered the phone after five rings, **and** he was very surprised to hear Joanna's voice.

> **Never use a comma alone to separate sentences.**

PRACTICE 2

Some of these compound sentences use commas correctly, but others use commas incorrectly to run sentences together. If the sentence is correct, write *OK* in the blank. Fix the run-on sentences. Add either a period and a capital letter, or add a conjunction (*and*, *but*, *so*) that fits the meaning of the sentence. The first one has been done for you.

_____ 1. Bill answered the phone, it was Joanna calling.

            Bill answered the phone. It was Joanna calling.
            or: *Bill answered the phone, and it was Joanna calling.*

_____ 2. She spoke softly, and Bill didn't know her voice at first.

_____ 3. Then he recognized her voice, he was surprised to hear from her.

_____ 4. They talked on the phone for hours, Joanna told him about her divorce.

_____ 5. They agreed to meet for coffee the next day, and coffee turned into candlelight dinner.

_____ 6. Bill was very happy to be with Joanna once more, Joanna fell in love with Bill all over again.

PROOFREAD

Remember all you have learned about when to use and when *not* to use commas. Correct the comma errors in this paragraph. You may need to add conjunctions to fix run-ons. There are ten mistakes in all, and the first one has been corrected for you.

        Bill wasn't rich, but he had a decent job. Joanna had her own job, *so*
she didn't need a man to support her. Joanna, looked at Bill with new eyes.
Bill was talented, exciting, and adventurous. Joanna admired, and cherished
him. They spent long hours on the phone, they talked about all of their
hopes, and dreams. Finally, Joanna, and Bill got married. Her new husband,
was not the perfect man, he left his dirty clothes on the floor, and he often
started arguments over little things. Joanna didn't mind too much, because
Bill showed his love in many ways, he let her live a happy life.

Answers start on page 178.

CUMULATIVE REVIEW

Show What You Know

People spend a lot of time thinking about the perfect man or woman. Most people wish they could find that ideal person. Of course, no one is perfect, but sometimes a person is lucky enough to find someone who makes him or her happy.

WRITING ASSIGNMENT

Choose *one* of the following topics and write two paragraphs of about six sentences each:

1. Describe the ideal husband or ideal wife. Think of the qualities this ideal person has. Think of background, personality, work history, income level, interests, and appearance.

2. Have you found a person who makes you happy (even if he or she is not perfect)? Write a paragraph about this person. You may discuss the person's background, personality, work history, income level, interests, or appearance.

In your paragraph, be sure to use commas correctly. When you are done writing, proofread carefully:

☑ There are no run-ons or fragments.
☑ You have put in commas where you need them.
☑ There are no unnecessary commas.

CHAPTER 9
MAKING SENTENCES
WORK TOGETHER

Goals

- To keep verb tenses consistent throughout a piece
- To make sure that every pronoun clearly refers to a noun
- To make sure that pronouns agree with the nouns they refer to

CHOOSING THE RIGHT TENSE

Write for the Moment

If a sentence is part of a paragraph or a longer piece of writing, it must work well with the other sentences in the piece. Take a look at the paragraph below. Notice especially the verbs. Do you see some problems? (For easy checking, each sentence has a number.)

> **(1)** Irma **has** a busy life and always **follows** the same routine. **(2)** Every morning, she **wakes** up at 6:00 and **takes** a shower. **(3)** Then she **got** dressed and **woke** up the children. **(4)** Next, she **made** breakfast for everyone. **(5)** She **checks** to see that the children **are** clean and neat. **(6)** She **watches** them go out the door, and then she **leaves** for work.

INSIGHT

A paragraph is a group of sentences about one topic or idea. Does this paragraph start with what Irma does *every day* or about what she did *yesterday*? _____ You're right if you said *every day*. The clues are in sentence 1 (*always*) and sentence 2 (*Every morning*). If the paragraph is about what Irma does every day, what verb tense should be used? (circle one)   **a.** present tense   **b.** past tense

You're right again if you said the *present tense* is used for things that happen every day.

Now look back at the paragraph. Did the writer use the present tense for every sentence about Irma's daily activities? _____ Which sentences need to be changed? Write the numbers here: _____ Sentences (3) and (4) use the past tense by mistake. Like the other sentences in the paragraph, sentences (3) and (4) should use the present tense.

Change the verbs in those sentences to the present tense:
Sentence (3) _____ Sentence (4) _____ You're right if
you wrote *gets dressed* and *wakes* for sentence (3) and *makes* for sentence (4). When
you are writing a paragraph, it is very important to keep the tense in mind.

- If you are talking about something that happens every day or is happening now, use the present.
- If you are talking about something that happened in the past, use the past tense.
- If you're talking about the future, use the future tense.

> **Use the correct tense for every sentence of a paragraph.**

PROOFREAD 1

Look at the clues in the first two sentences and decide what tense the paragraph should
use. Write *past, present,* or *future* on the line. Then check to be sure that every sentence
uses the correct tense. Cross out any wrong verbs and write the correct forms. There
are nine mistakes in all.

VERB TENSE: _____

Morris is a man of habit. Every weekend, he does the same things.
On Saturdays, he gets up early and cleans the bathroom. Then he went
downstairs, picked up the paper, and put on the coffee. He drinks his coffee
and reads the paper for several hours. At noon, he gets on the bus and
rode to the supermarket. There, he bought all the food he needed for the
week. Every Saturday night, he eats dinner in a restaurant with a good
friend, and then they went out to see a show. On Sundays, Morris spends
the morning at church and then visits his elderly mother. They always had
lunch together and played cards all afternoon. At the end of the day, Morris
goes home and eats supper. Every weekend is the same for Morris, but he
likes his routine.

PROOFREAD 2

Follow the directions for Proofread 1. There are eleven mistakes in all.

VERB TENSE: _____

Morris's mother had an interesting life when she was a young woman.
In 1920, she left her native land and came to this country. She learns English
quickly and found a job in a clothing factory. She was a talented singer

and dancer, and soon she finds a job on the stage. She starts out in the chorus, but soon she is singing and dancing the lead. She had a talent for comedy, and she tells jokes between the numbers. In her company, she met a young man with as much talent as she. They fall in love and get married. Soon they became a comedy team, and they travel around the country. They are very popular in their time. After several years, they started a family and decided to settle down in one place. They both get regular jobs, but they raise their children with a love of music and dance.

Answers start on page 179.

WRITING ASSIGNMENT
Choose *one* of the topics below.

1. Write a paragraph about a person you know. Think about the way this person lives now. Think about the person's habits, personality, and interests. Your paragraph should have at least eight sentences. Use the present tense throughout.

2. Write a paragraph about an unusual experience you had once. Think about an exciting thing you did or about a strange or frightening thing that happened to you. Your paragraph should have at least eight sentences. Use the past tense throughout.

Switching Tenses in a Paragraph

(1) Morris **lives** alone and **likes** his lifestyle. (2) Many years ago, he **was** married, but the marriage **broke** up after a short time. (3) Now, Morris definitely **prefers** the single life. (4) He **gets** up and **goes** to bed when he **wants** to. (5) He **goes** out or **stays** in as he **pleases**. (6) He **loves** his freedom.

Are all of the verbs above in the same tense? _____ Is this right or wrong? _____

The writer of the paragraph about Morris needed to talk about both the present and the past. This paragraph is mainly about the present—the way Morris lives now. For this reason, most of the sentences use the present tense. But sentence 2 goes back to the past to show how Morris's life has changed. Here, the writer had a good reason for changing to the past tense.

> **Change tenses only if you have a good reason to do so.**

PROOFREAD 3

Read this paragraph carefully. Pay close attention to the verb tenses. If there is a change in tense, make sure there is a good reason. If there is a *wrong* change in tense, correct the mistake. There are five mistakes in all, and the first one has been corrected for you.

As a young man, Morris married the young woman next door. Lilah **was** ~~is~~ bright, talented, and pretty. She played the piano and gave lessons. That piano drives Morris crazy. It bothered him when he was reading the paper or listening to the radio. In addition, Lilah always wanted to know where he was and what he was doing. Morris wanted out. Finally, he tells Lilah he is leaving. She agrees with his decision right away. Lilah later became a famous pianist, and she earned a lot of money. Nowadays, Morris looks back on his past with a little regret. After all, he is not rich or famous today. However, he is basically happy with his bachelor life.

Answers start on page 179.

CUMULATIVE REVIEW

Show What You Know

Have you ever read a story by a famous person about his or her life? A story like this is called an autobiography. Autobiographies tell about the most important things that happened to the person or that the person did.

WRITING ASSIGNMENT

Take a few moments and think back over some of the major events in your life. Then get ready to write your own autobiography. Of course, yours only needs to be three paragraphs long, so you can't tell everything!

First, list the most important events of your childhood years, your teenage or young adult years, and your life right now. Make this list of things you want to include before you begin to write your autobiography.

Then write your autobiography. Include a separate paragraph for each of the three periods of your life. (Remember to indent at the beginning of each paragraph.)

Use the correct tenses:

- past tense for past actions
- present tense for things that are happening now
- future for things that will take place later

Use transitions like *Next*, *After that*, and *Now* as you move from situation to situation.

When you are finished writing, proofread your work:

☑ All your sentences are complete.
☑ You have used commas correctly.
☑ Verb tenses are correct.
☑ Subjects agree with verbs.

PRONOUN WORK

The Mysterious *They*

Doctors serve us in different ways. **They** try to prevent and cure disease.

INSIGHT

Look at the **boldface** pronoun in the sentence above. Remember that a pronoun is a word that takes the place of a noun. What noun does the pronoun *they* stand for? _____ You're right if you wrote *doctors*. Check your answer by putting *doctors* in the place of *they*:

Doctors serve us in different ways. **Doctors** try to prevent and cure disease.

The sentence still makes sense. The word *doctors* in the first sentence is called an ***antecedent***. An antecedent is the word or group of words that a pronoun refers to. What happens if there is no antecedent? Take a look at the sentences below.

They are not doctors, but **they** do an important job. **They** prepare medicine for us.

After reading these sentences, do you feel a little confused? Whom is the writer talking about? Who are "they"? *They* has no antecedent, so there's no way of knowing. Take a look at the two sentences below. Here the writer has used the word *Pharmacists* instead of the first *They*. Now it is clear who is being written about.

Pharmacists are not doctors, but **they** do an important job. **They** prepare medicine for us.

> **Every pronoun must have an antecedent, a noun that it refers to.**

PRACTICE

Write a correct antecedent in each blank. Make sure the antecedent you choose makes sense. The first one has been done for you.

1. *Pharmacists* _____ are not doctors, but **they** do an important job. **They** prepare medicine for us.

2. _____ help doctors. In the past, **they** were almost all women, but nowadays **they** are sometimes men.

3. _____ fix our teeth. Many people are afraid of **them**.

4. My _____ operated on my heart. Thank goodness **she** did a wonderful job.

5. I take _____ for my heart. I must take **it** three times a day without fail.

6. In the hospital, I'm sharing a _____ with two other patients. **It** is sunny and bright.

7. Thank you for the beautiful _____! I love to look at **them** sitting there in the vase on the dresser.

8. My _____ came to see me last night. It was so nice of **him** to visit.

PROOFREAD 1

In the following passage, there are no antecedents—only pronouns. Your job is to supply the antecedents to make the sentences clear. Remember that not every pronoun needs to be taken out! You only need to put in enough antecedents so that the sentences are clear. Use each word below in the order given. The first one has been done for you.

doctors   people   patients   the doctor

Doctors
~~They~~ serve us in different ways. They try to cure and prevent disease.

They go to doctors when they are sick. They ask for help, understanding,

and advice.

They are sometimes unhappy with the treatment they receive. Some-

times they think that he is not good enough. Other times they feel he or

she does not listen carefully or answer important questions.

Now read over the passage to see if your changes make sense.

PROOFREAD 2

Follow the same directions as Proofread 1. Use the words below in the order they are given.

drugs   sick people   drug abuse
many hospitals   some companies and schools

They can be good or bad. They are good when they help them fight

disease. They are bad when they are abused.

It is a serious problem across the nation. It ruins lives. It even kills.

They have special drug abuse treatment programs. They have drug

counseling programs to help their workers or students. Fortunately, drug

abuse is decreasing.

Answers start on page 179.

PRONOUN AGREEMENT

Back to the Source

A security guard has to stand still for hours. However, **they** have to be ready for action at a moment's notice.

INSIGHT

There is a problem with the **boldface** pronoun above. Is the pronoun *they* singular or plural? _____ You're right if you said it's plural. Look back to the first sentence. See if you can find the words the pronoun *they* refers to (the antecedent). _____ _____ The writer clearly means *security guard* to be the antecedent. But wait. Is *security guard* singular or plural? _____ *Security guard* is singular, but *they* is plural. *They* cannot refer to *security guard*.

To fix this problem, you must change either the antecedent or the pronoun. Here are the two possible ways the sentences can be fixed. (Remember that subjects and verbs must agree.)

PLURAL: **Security guards have** to stand still for hours. However, **they have** to be ready for action at a moment's notice.

SINGULAR: **A security guard has** to stand still for hours. However, **he has** to be ready for action at a moment's notice.

> **A pronoun must agree with the noun it refers to.**
> **A singular pronoun agrees with a singular noun, and a plural**
> **pronoun agrees with a plural noun.**

PRACTICE 1

Choose the correct antecedent or pronoun from the words in parentheses. Write the word or words on the line.

1. A waiter needs a good memory. _____ must remember all of the orders. (*They/He*)

2. A waitress needs a lot of patience. _____ must deal with many personalities. (*They/She*)

3. _____ must have strong legs. They are on their feet all day long. (*Mail carriers/A mail carrier*)

4. _____ must be willing to risk his life. (*Policemen/A policeman*)

5. A businesswoman must work many hours at _____ desk. (*their/her*)

6. Pilots must limit _____ drinking for safety reasons. (*their/his*)

7. _____ should help people. People shouldn't be afraid to talk to them. (*Counselors/A counselor*)

8. Students must ask _____ which career is best. (*themselves/himself*)

Answers start on page 180.

More Work on Pronoun Agreement

1. **Students** should start studying early for tests. **You** shouldn't wait until the last moment.
2. **Students** should start studying early for tests. **They** shouldn't wait until the last moment.

Which pair of sentences is correct? _____ You're right if you said the second pair. Only use the pronoun *you* when speaking or writing directly *to* someone.

> **You** should start studying early for tests. **You** shouldn't wait until the last minute.

> **Use *you*, *your*, *yourself*, and *yourselves* as pronouns only when the antecedent is *you*.**

PRACTICE 2

Fill in the correct pronouns. First decide if you should use *they, them, themselves* or *you, yourself*.

Do you want to be a mail carrier? If so, _____ should re-
                                                         1
member this simple precaution. _____ should be careful around
                                               2
dogs. Do not assume that all of them will be nice to _____. Bring
                                                         3
some treats, and maybe _____ can make _____ a new
                          4   5
friend.

PROOFREAD

Find and correct the mistakes in pronoun usage in the paragraph below. Cross out the wrong words and write the correct word above. There are five mistakes in all, and the first one has been done for you.

Counselors have difficult jobs. ~~You~~ They must listen carefully to what your

clients have to say. People who go to counselors are trusting them to be

helpful and sympathetic. You must ask yourselves if you are focusing com-

pletely on the clients' lives.

Answers start on page 180.

CUMULATIVE REVIEW

Show What You Know

Has anyone ever asked for your advice? Imagine that you are asked to write advice for a popular magazine. In this assignment, you'll write two pieces, each with two paragraphs.

First, write two paragraphs about people. Each paragraph should have about six to eight sentences. In this piece of writing, use the pronouns *they, them,* and so on. (Do not use *you.*) Choose *one* of the following topics for your first piece of writing:

1. Write about parents of small children. Tell what parents should do to teach their children what is right and wrong. Tell how parents can encourage their children to learn.

2. Write about older or retired people. Tell what they can do to keep their lives full and enjoyable. Tell what they can do to keep themselves healthy.

In the second piece, you are asked to write two paragraphs each, this time writing your advice directly *to* someone. Each paragraph should have about six to eight sentences. This time, you will use the pronouns *you, your, yourself,* and so on. (Do not use *they.*) Choose *one* of the following topics for your second piece:

1. Write your advice to people who have just gotten married. Tell them what they can do to work out their problems and stay together.

2. Write your advice to a single man or woman. Tell this person how to make life full and enjoyable.

Check your paragraphs for the following:
- ☑ Subjects and verbs agree.
- ☑ All sentences are complete, and there are no fragments or run-ons.
- ☑ Adjectives and adverbs are used correctly.
- ☑ Transitions are used correctly.
- ☑ Pronouns agree with antecedents, and no pronoun is stuck without an antecedent.

FINAL TEST

This test covers the main points you have studied in this book. There are 100 points in all. There is no time limit on this test. After you have finished, check your answers on pages 164–65. The evaluation chart on page 165 will tell you in which areas you need to do additional work.

PART 1: VERB TENSES (12 points)

This conversation takes place at work between a boss and an employee named Jill. Circle the correct form of the verb in the parentheses. Make sure your answer makes sense with the rest of the passage. The first one has been done for you as an example.

BOSS: Good morning, Jill. Where (*is*/*are*) Fred today?

JILL: Bad news! He (*called*/*calls*) in about five minutes ago. He (*be*/*is*) in the hospital now!
  ₁ ... ₂

BOSS: What happened?

JILL: He (*had*/*having*) an accident last night. At around 7:00 he (*is riding*/*was riding*) his bicycle down Summit, and suddenly a car (*come*/*came*) by and knocked him down. Fortunately, two people (*was walking*/*were walking*) down the street at the time, and they (*got*/*was getting*) an ambulance for him.

BOSS: Tell me about Fred. Is he badly hurt?

JILL: Well, he (*resting*/*is resting*) comfortably now, but he (*will need*/*will needs*) an operation on his leg. He (*be*/*will be*) in the hospital for at least a week more.

BOSS: Do you have his number at the hospital? I (*want*/*wants*) to call him and speak to him about his sick leave. You know, we (*work*/*are working*) on that big project now, and I need to know if Fred will be able to finish it.

PART 2: *A* AND *AN*, PROPER NOUNS (4 points)

Read the paragraph and look for two types of mistakes:

- problems with *a* or *an*
- proper nouns that should be capitalized

Cross out each mistake and write the correct word(s) above. One has been done for you as an example.

I had ~~a~~ *an* accident last week, and now my doctor wants to operate on

my leg. I told doctor Weldus I wanted to avoid a operation. He gave me

the name of an specialist to call. Her office is in the town of fallingrock.

PART 3: QUESTIONS AND NEGATIVES (6 points)
Circle the correct group of words in the parentheses.

1. Where (*did you go/you go*) last night?
2. I didn't go (*nowhere/anywhere*).
3. Why (*you lying/are you lying*) to me?
4. I (*ain't/am not*) lying to you.
5. When (*will you stop/you stop*) lying to me?
6. You (*not be listening/are not listening*) to me.

PART 4: APOSTROPHES (10 points)
Add apostrophes only where they are necessary. Not every sentence needs an apostrophe.

1. The Smiths house is very neat.
2. However, the childrens room is a mess.
3. Their toys and clothes are all over the floor.
4. The mothers patience with her two boys is growing thin.
5. The boys habits have got to change.
6. Their parents want them to be more responsible.
7. Parents responsibilities can only go so far.
8. This shouldn't be a babysitters job either.
9. Many families yards are cluttered with toys.
10. Sometimes thieves take the babies playthings.

PART 5: PRONOUNS AND POSSESSIVES (8 points)
Write the correct pronoun in each blank.

Alicia and Ricardo are doing _____ best to run the household.
1

They are very proud of _____ son and daughter. He and _____ sister
2   3

are doing well in school. His best subject is math, and _____ is science.
4

Alicia is having trouble with the family car, however. Ricardo and _____
5

are constantly pouring water into the car, but _____ radiator leaks badly.
6

I will try to help them when they bring the car to _____ service station.
7

They can trust their car to my mechanics and _____.
8

PART 6: SINGULAR AND PLURAL NOUNS (6 points)

In this paragraph, look for mistakes in plural nouns. Cross out any mistakes and write the correct plural above. Watch out for irregular plurals. One has been done for you as an example.

Children
~~Childrens~~ are central to many family. Parent sacrifice many thing for

them. It is hard for some peoples to give so much and then see their children

grow up and leave. However, they must let them grow to become indepen-

dent mens and womans.

PART 7: ADJECTIVES AND ADVERBS (6 points)

Write the correct word on the line—adjective or adverb.

EXAMPLE: (*nasty/nastily*) Jimmy is a __nasty__ boy.

1. (*nasty/nastily*) He speaks to the girls very _____.
2. (*good/well*) He doesn't get along _____ with them.
3. (*serious/seriously*) He is not _____ about his schoolwork.
4. (*complete/completely*) The boys ignore him _____.
5. (*total/totally*) To them, Jimmy is a _____ fool.
6. (*immature/immaturely*) In fact, Jimmy is very _____.

PART 8: COMPARATIVE/SUPERLATIVE (8 points)

Decide which form is right for the sentence—comparative or superlative. Then write the correct form of the word in parentheses.

EXAMPLE: (*good*) In some ways, Japanese cars are __better__ than American cars.

1. (*carefully*) Many people think Japanese cars are made _____ than American cars.
2. (*cheap*) In addition, many Japanese cars are _____ than American cars.
3. (*expensive*) Of course, the _____ cars of all are neither Japanese nor American.
4. (*good*) In some ways, American cars are _____ than Japanese cars.
5. (*easily*) The owners of American models can fix their cars _____.
6. (*easy*) That's because it is _____ to reach different places in the engine than on Japanese cars.
7. (*safe*) When it comes to safety, the biggest cars are usually the _____ of all to drive.
8. (*spacious*) American cars tend to be _____ than Japanese cars.

PART 9: FRAGMENTS AND RUN-ONS (10 points)

Read each sentence. If it is correct, write *OK*. If it is not a complete sentence, write *frag*. Write *run-on* if it is a run-on. Rewrite the fragments or run-ons on a separate sheet to make complete, correct sentences.

EXAMPLE: __OK__ Many large cities have public transportation systems.

_____ **1.** They have subways they also offer bus service.

_____ **2.** Some people like to drive to work, but some prefer to take the bus.

_____ **3.** Some people get nervous driving in traffic, others hate waiting for the bus.

_____ **4.** For example, on a stormy day.

_____ **5.** Buses slow sometimes.

PART 10: COMMAS (10 points)

In the following paragraph, there are some commas, but more are needed. Add commas where they are necessary.

I look around me and I see many people. Some seem good and others seem bad. In my view, a "good" person is someone with no bad habits. This person doesn't smoke doesn't drink and doesn't use drugs. On the other hand, a "bad" person to me is someone with bad habits. This person may smoke drink use drugs and commit adultery. However, I must ask myself a question. Am *I* crystal clean? I must also consider the difference between a "good" person and a "bad" person. Maybe a man has no obvious vices but he is secretly cruel to his family. Maybe another man drinks too much but he saves a child from a burning building. I cannot always be sure about other people so I have to be careful in my judgments.

PART 11: SUBJECT-VERB AGREEMENT (10 points)

Read the passage and look for mistakes in subject-verb agreement. Cross out any verbs that do not agree with their subjects and write the correct verb above. One has been done for you as an example.

Managers in a company ~~has~~ *have* different responsibilities. A manager of experienced employees puts a lot of time into planning the work. This person don't supervise the workers very closely. However, a manager of new or unskilled workers spend more time overseeing the work. Of course, both a new worker and an experienced worker requires assistance from the manager, but the new worker probably needs more direct help. Each manager have a special style. Some managers act like dictators and gives orders without discussion. Other managers involve the workers in decisions. Everyone need to feel comfortable with the style of his or her manager.

New and experienced workers needs to know what is expected of them. There is problems when the boss does not make that clear. Maybe workers think everything is all right, but really work are not moving along fast enough. Future tension and trouble is avoidable if managers set clear goals.

PART 12: TENSE CHOICE, PRONOUN ANTECEDENTS, DOUBLE SUBJECTS (10 points)

Read this passage. Look for mistakes in verb tense and pronoun forms. Watch out for double subjects. Cross out the errors and write the correct form above. Two have been done for you as examples.

Rhonda ~~she~~ is a dental hygienist. She works for a dentist in a small office. Rhonda ~~had~~ *has* her own special duties, and she performed it carefully. Here is what happens when a typical patient visits Rhonda.

Very often, a nervous young man walks in. First, Rhonda tells them to sit down. She talks with the man and calmed him down. Then she always checks inside the patient's mouth for any signs of infection. After that, she began her most important job for the patient. She cleans his teeth carefully with special instruments. Finally, she tells them how to take care of their teeth in the future.

People often ask Rhonda about her job, and Rhonda she replies, "I felt good about my work. I help people keep the teeth you were born with."

Answers start on page 164.

Final Test Answer Key

PART 1: VERB TENSES

1. called
2. is
3. had
4. was riding
5. came
6. were walking
7. got
8. is resting
9. will need
10. will be
11. want
12. are working

PART 2: *A* AND *AN*, PRONUNCIATION FOCUS

Here is how the corrected paragraph should look:

I had **an** accident last week, and now my doctor wants to operate on my leg. I told **Doctor** Weldus I wanted to avoid **an** operation. He gave me the name of **a** specialist to call. Her office is in the town of **Fallingrock**.

PART 3: QUESTIONS AND NEGATIVES

1. did you go
2. anywhere
3. are you lying
4. am not
5. will you stop
6. are not listening

PART 4: APOSTROPHES

1. The Smiths' house is very neat.
2. However, the children's room is a mess.
3. no apostrophe
4. The mother's patience with her two boys is growing thin.
5. The boys' habits have got to change.
6. no apostrophe
7. Parents' responsibilities can only go so far.
8. This shouldn't be a babysitter's job either.
9. Many families' yards are cluttered with toys.
10. Sometimes thieves take the babies' playthings.

PART 5: PRONOUNS AND POSSESSIVES

1. They
2. their
3. his
4. hers
5. she
6. its
7. my
8. me

PART 6: SINGULAR AND PLURAL NOUNS

Here is how the corrected paragraph should look:

Children are central to many **families. Parents** sacrifice many **things** for them. It is hard for some **people** to give so much and then see their children grow up and leave. However, they must let them grow to become independent **men** and **women**.

PART 7: ADJECTIVES AND ADVERBS

1. nastily
2. well
3. serious
4. completely
5. total
6. immature

PART 8: COMPARATIVE/SUPERLATIVE

1. more carefully
2. cheaper
3. most expensive
4. better
5. more easily
6. easier
7. safest
8. more spacious

PART 9: FRAGMENTS AND RUN-ONS

These are samples of how the sentences may be corrected. Yours will probably be different. Have your instructor or a friend look over your work.

1. run-on — They have subways, and they also offer bus service.
2. OK
3. run-on — Some people get nervous driving in traffic. Others hate waiting for the bus.
4. fragment — For example, on a stormy day buses often run late.
5. fragment — Buses are slow sometimes.

PART 10: COMMAS

Here is how the corrected paragraph should look:

I look around me, and I see many people. Some seem good, and others seem bad. In my view, a "good" person is someone with no bad habits. This person doesn't smoke, doesn't drink, and doesn't use drugs. On the other hand, a "bad" person to me is someone with bad habits. This person may smoke, drink, use drugs, and commit adultery. However, I must ask myself a question. Am *I* crystal clean? I must also consider the difference between a "good" person and a "bad" person. Maybe a man has no obvious vices, but he is secretly cruel to his family. Maybe another man drinks too much, but he saves a child from a burning building. I cannot always be sure about other people, so I have to be careful in my judgments.

PART 11: SUBJECT-VERB AGREEMENT

Here is how the corrected passage should look:

Managers in a company **have** different responsibilities. A manager of experienced employees puts a lot of time into planning the work. This person **doesn't** supervise the workers very closely. However, a manager of new or unskilled workers **spends** more time overseeing the work. Of course, both a new worker and an experienced worker **require** assistance from the manager, but the new worker probably needs more direct help. Each manager **has** a special style. Some managers act like dictators and **give** orders without discussion. Other managers involve the workers in decisions. Everyone **needs** to feel comfortable with the style of his or her manager.

New and experienced workers **need** to know what is expected of them. There **are** problems when the boss does not make that clear. Maybe workers think everything is all right, but really work **is** not moving along fast enough. Future tension and trouble **are** avoidable if managers set clear goals.

PART 12: TENSE CHOICE, PRONOUN ANTECEDENTS, DOUBLE SUBJECTS

Here is how the corrected passage should look:

Rhonda ~~she~~ is a dental hygienist. She works for a dentist in a small office. Rhonda **has** her own special duties, and she **performs them** carefully. Here is what happens when a typical patient visits Rhonda.

Very often, a nervous young man walks in. First, Rhonda tells **him** to sit down. She talks with the man and **calms** him down. Then she always checks inside the patient's mouth for any signs of infection. After that, she **begins** her most important job for the patient. She cleans his teeth carefully with special instruments. Finally, she tells **him** how to take care of **his** teeth in the future.

People often ask Rhonda about her job, and Rhonda ~~she~~ replies, "**I feel** good about my work. I help people keep the teeth **they** were born with."

Final Test Evaluation Chart

Use the chart below to determine the grammar skills in which you need to do the most review. Write the total number of points for each part of the test and review areas where you missed half or more of the questions. Then add up the total number of points to find your final score.

Items	Review Pages	Points
Part 1 Verb Tenses	32–50	_____/12
Part 2 A and *An* Proper Nouns	24 22–23	_____/2 _____/2
Part 3 Questions and Negatives	52–65	_____/6
Part 4 Apostrophes	70–73	_____/10
Part 5 Pronouns Possessives	28–31 72–75	_____/2 _____/6
Part 6 Singular/Plural Nouns	25–27	_____/6
Part 7 Adjectives/Adverbs	79–86	_____/6
Part 8 Comparative/Superlative	87–96	_____/8
Part 9 Fragments Run-ons	115–19 127–31	_____/4 _____/6
Part 10 Commas	140–42, 145–47	_____/10
Part 11 Subject-Verb Agreement	97–113	_____/10
Part 12 Tense Choice Pronoun Antecedents Double Subjects	149–52 154–57 103	_____/4 _____/5 _____/1
	Total	_____/100

ANSWER KEY

CHAPTER 1: SENTENCE BASICS
UNDERSTANDING THE MESSAGE
PRACTICE, page 11
1. No   3. No   5. No   7. No
2. Yes   4. Yes   6. Yes   8. Yes
9. Your message should look like this:
   Your boss called. You won the company contest. You can get the prize now. The prize is a new radio.

TELLING OR ASKING?
PRACTICE, page 13
1. Helen is climbing over a wall.
2. What is she doing?
3. She is taking a test.
4. Why is she taking the test?
5. She wants to be a firefighter.
6. The test is hard.
7. Can she pass the test?
8. Do you think she will pass the test?
9. I think she will pass it.
10. She has always wanted to be a firefighter.
11. Was someone in her family a firefighter?
12. I think her father was one.

ACTION!
PRACTICE 1, page 14
Here are the six verbs that should be underlined: works, applied, got, cooks, makes, leaves.

PRACTICE 2, page 15
Here are the four verbs you should have underlined: is, worked, earns, are.

PRACTICE 3, page 15
1. stop   2. read   3. play   4. drink   5. listen
6. Answers will vary. Have your teacher or a friend look at your list to make sure all the words are really verbs.

THE ALIEN JUMPED OUT
PRACTICE 1, page 17
Here is how the paragraph should look:

The **alien** _was_ dead. **Parker** _called_ the other crew members. First **Collins** _arrived_ on the scene. Then **Davis** _ran_ into the room. **She** carefully _studied_ the dead alien. **Parker** _helped_ Davis. **Collins** _was_ too scared to do anything. Later, **Parker and Johnson** _opened_ the spaceship door. The **alien** silently _fell_ out into space. At last, the **spaceship** _was_ safe again.

PRACTICE 2, page 17
1. _Did_ the **alien** _live_ on another planet?
2. What _did_ the **alien** _eat_?
3. How _did_ **it** _enter_ the spaceship?
4. _Is_ **it** here now?
5. _Did_ **Parker** _kill_ it?
6. Where _are_ the other **aliens**?
7. What _was_ **Johnson** _doing_?
8. What _did_ **Davis** _discover_ about the alien?
9. How _did_ **Collins** _get_ a job on a spaceship?

THE OBJECT OF HER AFFECTION
PRACTICE 1, page 18
Here are the objects you should have circled:
1. Allen   4. cat   7. project
2. Allen   5. sister   8. job
3. cat   6. brothers

PRACTICE 2, page 19
Here is how the paragraph should look:

Amy _likes_ her fellow _workers_. **She** _loves_ _computers_, too. For this reason, her **job** _is_ fun. **She** _writes_ _programs_ all day. **She** also _supervises_ other _employees_. The **employees** _like_ _Amy_. **They** _talk_ to _her_ frequently. **She** _is_ helpful and patient.

SHOW WHAT YOU KNOW
PRACTICE 1, page 20
Here is how the conversation should look:
A: My name is Arnold.
   What is your name?
B: I'm Betty.
A: It's nice to meet you.
   What are you studying here?
B: I'm taking art classes.
   It's hard because I have a full-time job.
A: Where do you work?

B: I work in a video store.
   Are you working now?
A: No, I'm a full-time student.

PRACTICE 2, page 20

Here is how the paragraph should look:

       S   V   O   S   V   O
Betty has a full-time job. She also studies art.
          S V   O   S V
Every day, she draws pictures. Sometimes she paints,
       S   V   O   S   V
too. Her instructors like her work. They often display
    O   S V   V S
her pictures. Betty is very talented. Is she famous
     S   V   O
yet? No, she needs more practice first.

CHAPTER 2: NOUNS AND PRONOUNS

PEOPLE, PLACES, THINGS, IDEAS
PRACTICE 1, page 22

There is more than one correct answer for many of these. Have your teacher or a friend check that you used nouns correctly.

1. boy
2. girl
3. house (or apartment)
4. street (or avenue, road)
5. factory (or restaurant, gas station, etc.)
6. job (or position)
7. school (or college)
8. student

Here are the three other nouns (besides names) in the passage:

9. children
10. family
11. skills

PRACTICE 2, page 23

1. That road will take you to **Yates City**.
2. Take **Route 66** right into the center of town.
3. Turn left at the corner by the drugstore and **Slater's Shoes.**
4. My aunt and uncle live in a house on **Lilac Avenue**.
5. The cat and **Bowser** will probably be fighting when you get there.
6. Uncle Randy will yell to **Aunt Sophie** to call the vet.

PRACTICE 3, page 23

1. My **mother** wants me to visit Uncle Randy.
2. According to Mom, I don't keep in touch enough with my **relatives**.
3. However, my **dentist** says I can't go to Georgia next week.
4. Because Dr. Osmus wants to do a root canal right away, I can't travel out of **state** next week.

5. My sister Margo will help pay the **dental bill**.
6. My **brother** will go to Yates City in my place.

A LIFE OF AN EMPLOYEE
PRACTICE, page 24

1. an
2. a
3. a
4. an
5. an
6. a

ONE CAR, TWO CARS
PRACTICE 1, page 25

1. cars
2. pools
3. days
4. hours
5. boys
6. eggs
7. places
8. umbrellas

PRACTICE 2, page 26

1. toys
2. cities
3. dishes
4. churches
5. keys
6. parties
7. patches
8. brushes

PRACTICE 3, page 26

While your answers may vary, be sure to use plural nouns that make sense.

1. cars
2. rooms
3. tapes
4. watches
5. dresses
6. parties
7. boxes

WOMEN AND CHILDREN FIRST
PROOFREAD, page 27

Here is how the corrected paragraph should look. The corrected words appear in **boldface**.

    Children like to ask **questions** about everything. I know because I have three **children**—two **boys** and one girl. Here is an example. A few **weeks** ago, we were riding the bus. My daughter looked at two **women** in front of us. They were laughing at a joke. She said, "Mom, why are those two **people** laughing?" Then my baby boy asked, "Mom, when will I get all my grown-up **teeth**?" Next, my older boy said, "Mom, I saved five **dollars**. Can I buy some comic **books**?" It is hard to answer all their **questions**, but I try.

HE-MAN
PRACTICE, page 28

1. he
2. she
3. they
4. it
5. I
6. we
7. he

US AND THEM
PRACTICE 1, page 29

1. it
2. her
3. him
4. me
5. them
6. us

PRACTICE 3, page 30

1. us
2. They
3. He
4. us
5. we
6. him
7. She
8. She
9. we
10. her
11. We
12. them

PROOFREAD, page 31

Here is how the corrected paragraph should look:

My family and **I** have some good neighbors and some bad ones. I will tell you about the bad ones. **They** are very noisy. They fight all the time. I hear **them** every night. Also, the parents don't take care of their little girl. **She** is out on the street until midnight. The little boy usually stays out with **her.** The mother doesn't seem to mind. **She** and the father just ignore the children. Sometimes the children come to visit my children and **me. We** try to help them.

CHAPTER 3: VERBS
THE HERE AND NOW
PRACTICE 1, page 34

1. play
2. plays
3. likes
4. wants
5. go
6. stays
7. tell

PRACTICE 2, page 34

1. go
2. goes
3. has
4. have
5. does
6. do

PRACTICE 3, page 34

1. plays
2. has
3. have
4. call
5. dances
6. goes
7. watches
8. wants

PRACTICE 4, page 35

Your answers may be slightly different.
1. He plays baseball.
2. He plays for Boston.
3. He has a wife.
4. He has two children.
5. He has a cat.
6. He owns a two-story house.
7. He mows the lawn.

LOST AND FOUND
PRACTICE 1, page 36

1. called
2. picked
3. showed
4. counted
5. handed
6. thanked

PRACTICE 2, page 37

1. dropped
2. baked
3. dragged
4. fried
5. stayed
6. stopped
7. needed
8. applied

PROOFREAD, page 37

Correct answers are in **boldface**:

Yesterday, Sara **dropped** her garbage down the chute. She also **dropped** her wallet. She **screamed,** "Oh no!" The wallet **contained** $200, and Sara **needed** the money for the whole month. Sara **cried** for a few minutes, and then she **dried** her tears. She **returned** to her apartment, and she **planned** for the next month with no money. The next day, the janitor **phoned** with good news. Sara **jumped** with joy and **picked** up her wallet.

PRACTICE 3, page 39

You may have used different verbs from the list.

1. went
2. said
3. took
4. saw
5. lost (or left)
6. did
7. paid
8. got
9. left (or lost)
10. bought

PRACTICE 4, page 39

Here are some sample sentences. Yours may be slightly different.
1. John took a short trip.
2. John bought a used car.
3. John drove all the way to New York.
4. John saw the Statue of Liberty.
5. John rode the subway to Brooklyn.
6. John ate a delicious hot dog.
7. John drank a glass of stale beer.
8. John lost his driver's license.
9. John went to the police station.
10. John paid a stiff fine.
11. John finally got a new license.
12. John suddenly felt tired.
13. John left New York for good.

THE WILL TO SUCCEED
PRACTICE 1, page 40

Your sentences may look different from these. Have your instructor or a friend check to make sure you are using the future tense correctly.
1. She will be a happy person.
2. She'll be healthy.
3. She'll have many friends.
4. She will get a good education.
5. She will find a good job.
6. She'll have a wonderful family.

SHOW WHAT YOU KNOW
PROOFREAD, page 42

Here is how the corrected passage should look:

Ten years ago, Kelly's life was a mess. She **had** two **children**, but no job. She was divorced, and her boyfriend **treated** her badly.

Then her life **improved**. Why is she happy today? First, she got **an** education at night school. Then she got a job at **an** office. She met many new **friends** at work. She **told** her boyfriend good-bye. She became a strong **woman**.

Today, Kelly and her children **live** well. Her boy **has** all kinds of sports trophies. Her girl will **start** college in the fall. Also, Kelly met two nice **men** at school. Life isn't always easy, but she **laughs** a lot more than she used to.

THE STATE OF BEING
PRACTICE 1, page 43

1. am	3. is	5. are	7. are
2. is	4. are	6. is	8. am

YESTERDAY, WHEN I WAS YOUNG
PRACTICE 1, page 45

1. was	3. were	5. was
2. were	4. were	6. were

WHAT'S HAPPENING?
PRACTICE 1, page 46

1. is happening	4. is waiting
2. is stealing	5. are going
3. am watching	6. are wondering

PRACTICE 2, page 47

1. putting	5. running
2. taking	6. sleeping
3. picking	7. fleeing
4. stopping	8. flying

PROOFREAD, page 48

Correct answers are in **boldface**:

I **am** looking out my office window. I'm **watching** some workers while I **am** eating my lunch. The workers **are** building a new library for the city. They **are working** very hard. One worker is **driving** a cement truck. Another worker is **operating** a crane. Two more workers **are** drilling holes in the ground. I am **thinking** it would be fun to work with them. My three office friends **are** coming to the window. They **are** wondering what I **am** looking at.

WHAT WERE *YOU* DOING?
PRACTICE 1, page 50

1. was working	4. were giving
2. was trying	5. were sitting
3. were helping	6. were drinking

SHOW WHAT YOU KNOW
PROOFREAD, page 51

Here is how the corrected paragraph should look:

In 1980, Juan and Nilda Lopez **were living** in Mexico City. Juan was **an** office worker, and Nilda **was** a nurse. **They were** happy until Juan lost his job. Nilda was **working** night and day to support them both. Finally, Juan said, "I have a brother and two **sisters** in Texas. Let's go there."

Now they **are** living in Houston. Juan **is** working in a restaurant. He **is** unhappy with his job because his pay **is** too low. Nilda is **staying** home now. They **are studying** English at a church. They **are** learning more English every day. They **are working** hard for the future. They hope they **will** be happy again soon.

CHAPTER 4: MORE WORK WITH VERBS
DON'T GO AWAY!
PRACTICE 1, page 53

1. doesn't	5. doesn't
2. does not	6. does not
3. don't	7. do not
4. do not	

PRACTICE 2, page 53

1. Melvin doesn't love you.
2. You don't love Melvin.
3. Melvin doesn't care for you.
4. You don't know him very well.
5. Melvin does not earn enough money.
6. Melvin does not work hard.
7. Melvin does not have a good job.
8. I do not hate him.

I DIDN'T AND I WON'T!
PRACTICE 1, page 54

1. We didn't buy a BMW.
2. I didn't drive it dangerously.
3. I didn't park it on the street.
4. Jim and I didn't call our friends.
5. We did not give Aunt Tilly a ride.
6. We did not try the tape deck.
7. Jim did not break the mirror.
8. He did not take it to a service station.

PRACTICE 2, page 55

1. I won't do what you say.
2. I won't work hard at your gas station.
3. I won't work overtime without pay.
4. I will not wait until I'm thirty-five to get married.
5. I will not eat just beans and rice.
6. I will not drink only purified water.

I'M NOT GOING TO TAKE IT!
PRACTICE 1, page 56
1. am not
2. am not
3. is not
4. are not
5. was not
6. was not
7. were not

PRACTICE 2, page 57
1. You are not listening to me.
2. You are not telling the truth.
3. Joe is not working very hard.
4. He isn't treating his family well.
5. They aren't getting along fine.
6. We're not helping them enough.
7. I'm not meddling in their lives.

SHOW WHAT YOU KNOW
PRACTICE, page 58
Your answers may be slightly different. Have your instructor or a friend check to make sure you have used the verbs correctly.
1. had
2. was driving
3. looked
4. saw
5. wasn't moving
6. was making
7. slammed
8. jumped
9. said
10. didn't know
11. called
12. am calling
13. isn't moving
14. is making
15. won't stay
16. will miss
17. left
18. arrived
19. saw
20. doesn't talk
21. looks

NEGATIVE ATTENTION
PRACTICE 1, page 59
1. incorrect   There isn't no room for mistakes.
2. correct   We don't have any problems.
3. correct   She never goes anywhere alone.
4. incorrect   They didn't see nothing in the room.
5. correct   There are no bugs in this house.
6. incorrect   Don't you have no brothers and sisters?
7. correct   Does no one want my advice?
8. incorrect   I can't get no satisfaction.

PRACTICE 2, page 60
1. We don't have **any** time for that.
2. There **is** nothing in my pockets.
3. I have **no** idea where she is.
4. I'm not **a** millionaire.
5. There **aren't** any good shows on TV tonight.
6. **No one** is in the room—it's empty.
7. Please don't tell me **anything** bad about him.
8. He doesn't have **an** opinion on that.

PROOFREAD, page 60
Here is an example of how the corrected passage might look. Yours might be slightly different.

Kathy left Jeff because he never did **anything** nice for her. He didn't buy her **any** flowers, and he didn't do **any** housework. In fact, he never did **anything** to help her. However, he saw nothing wrong with his behavior.

When Kathy left, Jeff was hungry because there **was** no food in the house. The house got dirty because no one cleaned it. In time, he learned to shop and to clean, but he still didn't have **anyone** to talk to. He thought, "There **isn't anyone** for me to care about. There wasn't **anybody** as nice as Kathy. I can't get **anywhere** in life without her."

So Jeff called up Kathy and told her he never meant her **any** harm. Kathy gave Jeff another chance, and they're together today. Jeff **isn't** perfect, but now he does his best.

ASK ME ANYTHING
PRACTICE 1, page 61
1. **Do** you **like** jazz?
2. What kind of music **do** you **like**?
3. **Does** Rhonda **have** a stereo?
4. What kind of stereo **does** she **have**?
5. Where **does** she **keep** her stereo?
6. **Do** Rhonda and Jerry **like** to dance?
7. How often **do** they **give** parties?

PRACTICE 3, page 62
Here is a list of all the questions Tonya should ask. Yours may vary slightly.
1. Where does he live?
2. Does he have a job?
3. What kind of music does he like?
4. What kind of movies does he like?
5. Does he have any hobbies?
6. What does he look like?
7. Does he have a girlfriend?

ARE YOU LONESOME TONIGHT?
PRACTICE 1, page 64
1. were
2. are
3. are
4. Were
5. Was
6. Is

PRACTICE 2, page 64
1. How are you?
2. Is Bobby at home?
3. Where was he yesterday?
4. Were they in a fight?
5. Why is he still mad?
6. Were you scared?

PRACTICE 3, page 65
Your questions may vary slightly.
1. Where is she standing?
2. What is she doing?
3. What is she eating?
4. What is she wearing?
5. Where is she going?
6. Why is she coming over here?

SHOW WHAT YOU KNOW
PRACTICE 1, page 66
1. **Do** they **like** to hunt?
2. **Are** they **hunting** right now?
3. **Are** the children **sleeping** now?
4. **Do** they **sleep** eight hours every night?
5. What **does** Mary **do** after school every day?
6. Were you **reading** when I came home last night?

CHAPTER 5: NOUN AND PRONOUN FOCUS
WATER, WATER EVERYWHERE
PRACTICE 1, page 68
1. count
2. noncount
3. count
4. noncount
5. noncount
6. count
7. noncount
8. count
9. noncount
10. noncount
11. count
12. noncount

PRACTICE 2, page 68
1. look
2. looks
3. smells
4. feel
5. sounds
6. look
7. is
8. gets

PRACTICE 3, page 69
1. few
2. many
3. much
4. few
5. little

FRANCO'S WAGES
PRACTICE 1, page 70
1. This is **someone's** money.
2. I think it is **LaTisha's** money.
3. **Franco's** wages are very good.
4. The **company's** pay scales are very high.
5. His **wife's** salary is too low.
6. Her **supervisor's** wages are also low.
7. The **family's** income is all right.

PRACTICE 3, page 71
1. The **Browns'** two daughters are smart.
2. The **girls'** math homework is better than the other **students'** work.
3. The **Browns'** two sons are also bright.

4. The **boys'** reading work is better than their **classmates'** work.
5. Their math and reading **teachers'** reports are always good.

PRACTICE 4, page 72
1. People's
2. men's
3. women's
4. women's
5. children's

PROOFREAD, page 73
Here is how the corrected paragraph should look:
Sometimes it is hard for **adults** to be in school. This is because adults are often **parents** and **workers** as well as **students.** An **adult's** life can be too full of **worries** about home and work.

PROOFREAD, page 73
Here is how the corrected paragraph should look:
Martin **Chang's** job is a good one. Mr. **Chang's** salary is $20,000. Mr. Chang has three female **helpers.** The **helpers'** wages are much lower. Mr. Chang's wife has a lot to say about this. She thinks the **women's** pay is too low. Mr. Chang disagrees with his **wife's** opinion. He thinks people's **salaries** depend on their jobs. He thinks his **assistants'** pay is fair.

YOURS, MINE, AND OURS
PRACTICE 2, page 75
1. Your children are grown up, but **mine** are still young.
2. Your son has his friends, and your daughter has **hers.**
3. This old car is **ours.**
4. My neighbors' dogs are huge, but **mine** are small.
5. My dogs are poodles, and **theirs** are German shepherds.
6. That is not my problem. It is **yours**!

SEE FOR YOURSELF
PRACTICE, page 77
1. I am looking at myself.
2. She is talking to herself.
3. The children are drawing pictures of themselves.
4. Sally and I are shopping for ourselves.
5. He is taking a picture of himself.
6. You are working for yourselves.
7. It is scratching itself.

SHOW WHAT YOU KNOW
PROOFREAD, page 78

Here is how the corrected paragraph should look:

At holiday time, my neighborhood looks like a carnival. In December, my next-door **neighbors** put colored **lights** in **their** windows. Across the street, the **Robinsons'** yard is decorated with two **Santas** and one giant reindeer. The **reindeer's** nose is a bright red lightbulb, and **its** tail is a white lightbulb. Down the block, Mrs. **Smith's** roof is covered with Santa Claus, **Santa's** sleigh, and several yellow **stars.** The fat elf by the driveway is **hers**, too. The **Hendersons'** front yard has a huge Christmas tree. Everyone else has a regular green tree, but **theirs** is pink and white! **My** apartment is very plain. Other **people's** windows are full of lights and tinsel, but **mine** just have curtains. I guess that is why my **neighbors** call me Mr. Scrooge!

CHAPTER 6: ADJECTIVES AND ADVERBS
THE BEAUTIFUL PEOPLE
PRACTICE 1, page 80

1. Jessica is a **good** actress.
2. She is **beautiful.**
3. Robert is **handsome**.
4. He is a **famous** actor.
5. He looks **sensational.**
6. Robert is a **rich** man.
7. Do you know any **real** actors?

OH, REALLY?
PRACTICE 1, page 81

1. Mark speaks **softly** to his children.
2. He **carefully** listens to their problems.
3. He **clearly** explains the rules.
4. The children look at their father **respectfully.**
5. They answer him **politely.**
6. Most of the time, they **happily** obey him.

PRACTICE 2, page 82

Your sentences may be worded slightly differently.
1. Stella treats her children unkindly.
2. She speaks nastily to her children.
3. The children talk to her rudely.
4. The children look at their mother disrespectfully.
5. The children behave badly.
6. The children fight noisily.

REAL NICE OR REALLY NICE?
PRACTICE 1, page 85

1. ADJ. Mrs. Stone is a **good** person.
2. ADV. She speaks **kindly.**
3. ADJ. She is **polite**.
4. ADV. She treats people **politely**.
5. ADV. Mrs. Stone is **really** thoughtful.
6. ADJ. Mrs. Stone is a **careful** listener.
7. ADJ. She is a **good** singer.
8. ADV. She sings **well.**

PROOFREAD, page 86

Here is how the corrected paragraph should look:

My parents left when I was **really** young, so I lived with my grandmother. She took good care of me, and she raised me **well.** She had a **really** quiet voice, and she always talked to me **softly.** I liked to listen to her because she always spoke to me **seriously**, but she was never unkind. I lived **happily** with her until I grew up. She **peacefully** died a few years ago, but I still remember her **well.**

THE BIGGER THE BETTER
PRACTICE 1, page 88

1. Baltimore is smaller than New York.
2. New York is larger than Chicago.
3. Los Angeles is sunnier than New York.
4. Vancouver is rainier than Los Angeles.
5. Miami is hotter than New York.
6. Phoenix is newer than Boston.
7. Los Angeles is smoggier than Kansas City.
8. Answers will vary. Check with your instructor or a friend to make sure you used *better* correctly.

PRACTICE 2, page 89

1. New York is more crowded than Santa Fe.
2. Chicago is more polluted than Santa Fe.
3. Boston is more historic than Dallas.
4. New York is more famous than Spokane.
5. Detroit is more industrial than Miami.
6. Miami is more tropical than Toronto.

PROOFREAD, page 89

Here is how the corrected paragraph should look:

Let's compare two cities: Toronto and Las Vegas. First, Toronto's weather is **worse** than the weather in Las Vegas. It is much ~~more~~ colder and **snowier** than Las Vegas. In cultural life, Toronto is **more famous** for its museums and concerts. Las Vegas is ~~more~~ smaller than Toronto, but if you like gambling, it is a ~~more~~ **better** place to be.

THE BEST IS YET TO COME
PRACTICE 1, page 91
1. Chicago is the windiest city.
2. New York is the largest city.
3. Phoenix is the sunniest city.
4. Philadelphia is the most historic city.
5. Detroit is the most industrial city.
6. Seattle is the rainiest city.
7., 8. Answers will vary. Have your instructor or a friend look over your sentences to be sure you used *the best* and *the worst* correctly.

PRACTICE 3, page 92
Comparative	Superlative
1. taller	the tallest
2. prettier	the prettiest
3. more beautiful	the most beautiful
4. stronger	the strongest
5. more surprising	the most surprising
6. chubbier	the chubbiest
7. better	the best
8. worse	the worst

PROOFREAD, page 92
Here is how the corrected paragraph should look:
    I have three sisters. Jackie is the ~~most~~ oldest. She is also the **most** musical of all three. Meg is the ~~most~~ youngest. In some ways, she is **more intelligent** than Jackie. She is the **best** student of all, but she is the **worst** cook. Wilga is a ~~more~~ better cook than Meg. Each sister has something she does the **best**.

SEEING MORE CLEARLY
PRACTICE, page 95
1. worst
2. faster
3. more recklessly
4. harder
5. best
6. fastest
7. better
8. more cautiously
9. the most carefully

PROOFREAD, page 95
Here is how the corrected paragraph should look:
    Biff's life was **more difficult** after the accident. He had to walk much more **slowly** than before. He couldn't do his old job, and his new job was much **worse** than the old one. He became much **more serious**, and some of his friends deserted him. But in some ways his life became ~~more~~ better. Before the accident, he was the ~~most~~ fastest driver of all his friends. Afterwards, he became the ~~most~~ safest. He used to act without thinking, but now he thought more **carefully** before he acted. He began to behave more **maturely**. Even though his life was harder, he decided he would always try his **best**.

CHAPTER 7: AGREEMENT
REVIEW OF SUBJECTS AND VERBS
PRACTICE, page 98
1. *subject*: I
   verb: am working
2. *subject*: I
   verb: scrape
3. *subject*: family
   verb: helps
4. *subject*: They
   verb: don't fry
5. *subject*: They
   verb: are making
6. *subject*: son
   verb: was scrubbing
7. *subject*: I
   verb: wonder
8. *subject*: hood
   verb: has
9. *subject*: It
   verb: didn't bother
10. *subject*: mother
   verb: came

LET'S AGREE ON SOMETHING
PRACTICE, page 99
1. lives
2. doesn't
3. am
4. don't
5. are
6. drink
7. is
8. doesn't
9. were
10. don't
11. was
12. wasn't

THE KING AND I
PRACTICE 1, page 101
1. no comma
2. Ryan, Jane, and I need a doctor.
3. no comma
4. My head, my ears, and my throat hurt.
5. Cold weather, bad food, and a late night caused us to get sick.
6. no comma

PRACTICE 2, page 101
1. Ryan and I look bad.
2. Ryan, Jane, and I need a doctor.
3. Ryan, Jane, and I are coughing.
4. Pills, vitamins, and cough syrup are expensive.
5. Children and old people get sick easily.
6. Good nutrition and bed rest are important for sick people.

PRACTICE 3, page 102
1. Ryan, Jane, and **I** stayed out too late last weekend.
2. OK
3. **Ryan and I** had too much to drink.
4. **My brother and I** stayed out until dawn.
5. **He and I** didn't get home until six in the morning.
6. OK
7. Our parents and **she** got angry with us.
8. **They** and my grandmother were worried about us.
9. OK

DOUBLE TROUBLE
PROOFREAD, page 103

Here is how the corrected paragraph should look:

My brother Joe plays guitar in a band. He also sings back-up. The other band members ~~they~~ sing too. Of course, the band members ~~they~~ also play their instruments—keyboard, bass, and drums. The drummer ~~he~~ is very talented. He and my brother ~~they~~ want to start a new band together.

SEPARATION ANXIETY
PRACTICE 1, page 104

1. A mother ~~with triplets~~ has her hands full.
2. A father ~~with five children~~ is always busy.
3. The baby ~~of the family~~ is sometimes spoiled.
4. Sometimes parents ~~of teenagers~~ are not strict enough.
5. Teenagers ~~in a large family usually~~ want more privacy.
6. The people ~~next door to me~~ have teenage triplets.
7. The boys ~~next door~~ share one room.
8. One ~~of them~~ goes to a special school.

PRACTICE 2, page 105

1. Parents of any child **have** a big responsibility.
2. A child with loving parents **is** lucky.
3. Most children with special problems **need** special care.
4. Often, the parents of a disabled child **are** not prepared for the expense.
5. A teacher of retarded children **has** to be patient.
6. A program for children with special problems **requires** help from the parents.

PRACTICE 3, page 105

1. The child next door ~~she~~ is deaf.
2. The parents of this little girl ~~they~~ love her very much.
3. The mother of the family ~~she~~ speaks sign language well.
4. The father of the family ~~he~~ is trying to learn it.
5. The school in the neighborhood ~~it~~ has special classes for deaf children.
6. The teacher of one of these classes ~~he~~ is helping the parents.

PROOFREAD, page 106

Here is how the corrected passage should look:

Crime in the streets **is** a serious problem in modern cities. Robberies, rapes, and muggings **happen** every day. Experts give different reasons for crime.

Unemployment in the cities **is** certainly a major cause. People without a job **do** not have enough money. In addition, they are angry and frustrated. Often, anger and frustration **lead** to crime.

Gangs **are** another problem. Young men and even young women **join** gangs because they have no other choice. A gang of boys **forces** another boy to join by threatening to kill him. Fights between one gang and another **are** responsible for much crime in the street.

Sometimes violence in the home causes crime on the streets. A child of violent parents **learns** to be violent himself. Beatings and other kinds of violent punishment **teach** a child that it is OK to hurt other people.

Crime in the streets **hurts** everyone. To stop it, the school, the government, and the family **need** to work together.

EVERYTHING AND NOTHING
PRACTICE 1, page 108

1. is
2. is
3. seems
4. makes
5. worries
6. is

PRACTICE 2, page 109

1. My favorite pair of pants **is** caught in a bicycle chain.
2. These scissors **are cutting** you free.
3. Don't do that! These trousers **are** my best pair!
4. That old pair of jeans **belongs** in the trash.
5. Your dirty pair of glasses **makes** everything look bad.
6. My clothes **were** the best that money can buy.

PRACTICE 3, page 110

1. looks
2. is
3. are
4. gets
5. has
6. makes

PROOFREAD, page 110

Here is how the corrected passage should look:

Problems with money **are** major troubles in someone's life. If someone **doesn't** have enough money, he or she cannot pay for food, rent, clothing, and other things. Good, cheap food **becomes** hard to find. Clothes **get** torn and shabby looking.

The solution to money problems **is** to find a good job. However, not everyone **is** able to do this.

People without work **have** to depend on the government for support. No one **gets** rich on government money.

HERE'S JOHNNY!
PRACTICE 1, page 111
1. There **is** more <u>juice</u> in the refrigerator.
2. OK
3. There **are** <u>glasses</u> right at the edge of the table.
4. OK
5. Here **sits** the <u>hostess</u> of the party.
6. There **are** <u>fun and games</u> still to come.
7. OK
8. There **goes** your <u>wife</u>.

PRACTICE 2, page 112
1. There is a bottle on the table.
2. There is some wine in the bottle.
3. There are some glasses on the table.
4. There isn't any wine in the glasses.
5. There is a bag on the table.
6. There aren't any doughnuts in the bag.
7. There are some taco chips in the bag.
8. There is some onion dip in the jar.
9. There isn't any cheese on the table.
10. There isn't any ice cream on the table.

PROOFREAD, page 113
Here is how the corrected paragraph should look:

In my kitchen, **there** is only one cabinet. There is a lot of food in it. There **are** two jars of jelly. There **are** four cans of soup. **There** is a box of cereal. There are five bottles of salad dressing. There **are** some spices, too, but there **isn't any** sugar. There isn't **any** salt, either. I have to buy a pound of sugar and a pound of salt.

CHAPTER 8: WRITING CORRECT AND COMPLETE SENTENCES
SOMETHING IS MISSING
PRACTICE 1, page 116
1. A <u>smoke bomb</u> **exploded**.
2. A <u>man</u> with a beer can <u>threw</u> it.
3. <u>He</u> was drunk.
4. His <u>team</u> was losing.
5. The <u>police</u> arrested the drunk man.

PRACTICE 2, page 116
1. verb 4. verb
2. subject 5. verb
3. subject

PRACTICE 3, page 117
1. fragment—subject 6. sentence
2. sentence 7. fragment—subject
3. sentence 8. sentence
4. fragment—verb 9. fragment—subject
5. fragment—subject 10. fragment—verb

PROOFREAD, page 119
Here is how the corrected paragraph should look:

Families often fight over the television. The father likes football. The mother of the family likes professional golf. The little children like cartoons. Everybody argues. The winner of the argument watches his favorite show. The losers of the argument must do something else.

MEANWHILE, BACK AT THE RANCH
PRACTICE, page 120
Here is an example of how the corrected paragraph should look. You may have used different transition words.

Larry is a shoe salesman. He arrives at work at 9:00. **First,** he talks to his boss. **Next,** he works on the shoe displays. **For instance,** he might put a new set of shoes in the window. He opens the doors at 10:00. **Then** he helps the customers all day long. Larry locks the doors at 6:00. **Then** he helps the boss clean up.

SHOW WHAT YOU KNOW
PROOFREAD, page 121
Here is how the corrected paragraph should look.

I'd like to tell you about our neighborhood. ~~Have~~ We have many service businesses ~~on~~ in this area. For example, you will find dry cleaners, shoe repairs, and laundromats. In addition, there are many retail stores. For instance, shoe stores, dress shops, and supermarkets. You can ~~Can~~ also find a few factories. There are two ~~Two~~ clothing factories and a pizza factory. Our neighborhood ~~It~~ is good for business.

COMPOUNDING THE INTEREST
PRACTICE 1, page 122
1. It rained for three days, and the river flooded.
2. Water filled the streets, and people used boats instead of cars.
3. Parents left their jobs, and children left their schools.
4. Some people stayed with friends, and others went to shelters.

5. The army came to help, and the National Guard joined in.
6. Mr. Brown lost his store, and Mrs. Jones lost her house.
7. The people rebuilt the town, and the government helped.

PRACTICE 3, page 123

1. Cocaine is dangerous, but many people use it.
2. Cocaine is expensive, but many people buy it.
3. Marijuana is illegal, but many people smoke it.
4. Cigarettes are harmful, but many people smoke them.
5. People read about the dangers, but they don't pay attention.

PRACTICE 4, page 124

1. The baby was crying, so his father picked him up.
2. The baby was hungry, so his mother fed him.
3. He was sick, so his father took him to the clinic.
4. He was wet, so his mother changed him.
5. He smiled, so his mother ran for the camera.

PRACTICE 5, page 124

Here is an example of a corrected paragraph. Yours may look slightly different.

Bonnie and Jack Randall had a drinking problem, **but they** didn't realize it. Every day Bonnie drank a bottle of wine, **and** Jack drank five martinis. They started to lose all of their friends, **but** they didn't seem to care. One day, Jack showed up at work drunk, **so** his boss fired him. Jack told Bonnie about it, **and** they finally decided to get some help from Alcoholics Anonymous. The Randalls are trying hard to change their lives.

BECAUSE I SAID SO!
PRACTICE 1, page 125

1. Claudia stayed home because her son was sick.
2. She was worried because he had a high fever.
3. She took him to the clinic because he had a terrible earache.
4. Claudia's boss was upset because she was absent from work.
5. Claudia's husband stayed home the next day because Claudia couldn't miss any more work.

PRACTICE 2, page 125

1. Claudia missed a day of work, and her boss got angry.
2. She returned to work the next day because she was afraid of losing her job.
3. Rafael stayed with their son because he had the day off.
4. The boy got better, so Rafael went back to work the following day.
5. The little boy felt much better, so he returned to school.

6. Claudia was relieved because her son was well again.
7. The little boy recovered completely, but Rafael got sick.
8. He went to bed, and Claudia called the clinic again.
9. Claudia was exhausted, but she didn't get sick.
10. She felt lucky because she stayed well.

RUNNING OFF AT THE MOUTH
PRACTICE 1, page 127

1. Many teenage girls drop out of school. They leave to have babies.
2. These girls are very young. Some of them are under fifteen.
3. A teenage mother can lose her freedom. She can also lose her education.
4. A teenage mother can finish her education. It is difficult, though.

PRACTICE 2, page 129

1. run-on   Education is important it can be difficult.
2. OK   Education is important, but it is often hard.
3. run-on   Some people quit school they lose their education.
4. OK   Sometimes they change their minds, and they go back to school.
5. run-on   Some people return to high school others get their GED.
6. run-on   An education gives you basic skills it also gives you the chance for a decent job.
7. OK   A diploma is not a guarantee, but it can help you.
8. OK   A diploma means hard work. The effort is worth it.

PRACTICE 3, page 129

Here is how the corrected paragraph should look:

Young people drop out of high school for different reasons. **One** reason is problems in the school. Some schools are dangerous. **They** are full of gangs. Serious students are often afraid to come to school, and they quit. In addition, some young women get pregnant. **They** soon leave to give birth to their babies. **The** babies need care, so the mothers don't want to leave them.

PRACTICE 4, page 130

Your answers may vary. Have an instructor or a friend look over your work to make sure you have fixed the run-ons correctly.

1. Karen was seventeen years old, **and** she was nine months pregnant.
2. She wanted her baby, **but** she also wanted her education.
3. She wanted to stay in school, **but** she had to leave.
4. Karen had a baby boy, **and** she loved him very much.
5. She didn't have enough money, **so** she couldn't give him many toys or clothes.
6. She wanted a job, **but** she couldn't find one.
7. She wanted to go back to school, **but** she didn't want to leave her baby alone.
8. She wanted to give her son plenty of opportunities, **so** she wanted to further her own education.

PROOFREAD, page 130

Here is an example of how the corrected paragraph might look. Your answers may vary somewhat. Have your instructor or a friend check to make sure you have fixed the run-on sentences.

Karen talked to a friend in her neighborhood. **Her** friend told her about a special school program for teenage mothers. The school has a day-care center right in the building, **so** the young mothers can bring their children to school. The children are cared for, **and** the mothers can study at the same time. Karen joined the program. **She** is very pleased with it. She brings her son to the day-care center in room 101. **Then** she goes to room 202 for her classes. Karen is taking a class in child care **because** she wants to learn how to be a better mother. She also works for a program for other teenagers in the high school. **In** this program she tells them to wait before having a baby.

REVIEW: FRAGMENTS AND RUN-ONS
PRACTICE 1, page 131

1. OK   Frank is a student at Weller High, (and) he is doing well.
2. frag   He a good student now.
3. frag   Gets good grades in school.
4. run-on He studies hard he is also active in sports.
5. OK   He plays on the school soccer team.

6. run-on This year he is happy last year he wasn't.
7. frag   Last year had a problem with drugs.
8. run-on His friends were using crack he wanted it too.
9. frag   Didn't want to seem different.
10. OK   His grades went down, (and) he stopped attending school.
11. OK   Then a school counselor talked to Frank.
12. frag Convinced Frank to join an anti-drug program.
13. frag Was hard, (but) Frank gave up the drugs.
14. run-on Frank is repeating tenth grade this time he is doing well.
15. frag Frank a lucky young man.

EAT, DRINK, AND BE MERRY
PRACTICE 1, page 133

1. The audience clapped and whistled.
2. The band bowed and played another song.
3. The lead singer sang and shouted.
4. The back-up singers sang and danced.
5. The guitarists played and jumped up in the air.
6. The drummer beat out a rhythm and played a solo.
7. The people sang along and danced in the aisles.

PRACTICE 2, page 134

1. The audience clapped enthusiastically, whistled loudly, and shouted.
2. The band smiled, bowed, and left the stage.
3. We put on our coats, picked up our bags, and left the concert hall.
4. We got in the car, drove to a restaurant, and ordered a pizza.
5. We ate two pizzas, drank two pitchers of cola, and talked for three hours.
6. I went home, put on my pajamas, and fell asleep right away.

PRACTICE 3, page 135

1. Maria sings and **plays** the piano.
2. She often writes and **performs** her own music.
3. She thinks up the melody, tries it out, and **writes** it down.
4. Maria's parents love their daughter and **respect** her talent.

5. They read her songs, listen to her music, and **are** very proud of her.

6. Maria **sings** well and hopes for a successful future in music.

PRACTICE 4, page 136

1. The baby was screaming and **crying**.
2. The father picked him up and **offered** him a bottle.
3. His baby **drank** the milk and smiled happily.
4. Babies often scream and **cry**.
5. They want to eat and **get** attention.
6. A comfortable baby will shut its eyes and **fall** asleep.
7. Parents know and **respond** to their baby's needs.
8. Does a good parent always know and **respond** correctly?
9. Even a good parent will misunderstand and **make** a mistake sometimes.
10. When you were a child, your parents **fed** you and gave you attention.
11. You needed food and also **wanted** love.

JOANNA, ZACK, AND BILL
PRACTICE 2, page 141

1. **Zack** and **Bill** wanted to marry Joanna.
2. Zack was **handsome, rich,** and **elegant.**
3. Bill was **intelligent** and **kind.**
4. Zack gave Joanna **diamonds, rubies,** and **emeralds.**
5. Bill sent Joanna **small pictures** and **love letters.**
6. Joanna wanted **money, respect,** and **love.**
7. Bill **loved, helped,** and **talked to** her.
8. Bill **helped Joanna with her career, talked to her about her problems,** and **promised eternal love.**
9. Zack offered **money** and **prestige.**
10. After their wedding, **Joanna** and **Zack** argued all the time.
11. Joanna **thought for a long time** and **made up her mind.**
12. Joanna **gave up Zack** and **married Bill.**

PROOFREAD, page 142

Here is how the corrected paragraph should look:
    Joanna wanted love, but she also wanted money. A rich man proposed to her, and she thought she'd find happiness with him. He promised her fast cars, fine wine, and fancy clothes. He delivered his promises, but he didn't make Joanna happy. The gifts were exciting, but the man wasn't. The rich man was quiet, boring, and unadventurous. He had wanted her to stay home, so she had quit her job. Joanna became lonely, bored, and frustrated. The expensive clothes, the beautiful house, and the elegant furniture were not enough for Joanna.

THINKING, WRITING, AND FIXING
PRACTICE 1, page 143

1. OK
2. Bill's hobbies were playing saxophone, shooting baskets, and (to skydive.)
3. Bill was good at passing, dribbling, and (to get) rebounds.
4. OK
5. Bill's job was routine, dull, and (had few events.)
6. However, he got good pay, plenty of vacation, and (took) a few personal days.
7. Bill enjoyed traveling, meeting people, and (adventurous.)
8. His life was interesting and (rewards.)

PRACTICE 2, page 144

Here are some examples of how the sentences can be fixed. Yours may look slightly different.

1. At her job, Joanna set up displays of new records, tapes, and **compact discs.**
2. Joanna managed the staff and **worked** noon to eight P.M.
3. She also liked hobbies that were adventurous, active, and **fun.**
4. She enjoyed playing piano, mountain climbing, and **taking** photographs.
5. She used her savings to buy a motorcycle and **to take** a trip around the country.
6. She always rode carefully and **cautiously.**
7. Money can't guarantee adventure, fun, and **excitement.**

OVERDOING IT
PRACTICE 1, page 146

1. Joanna ✗ was married to Zack for five years.
2. OK
3. The marriage of her dreams ✗ turned into a prison.
4. She wanted her own career ✗ and a happy life.
5. She finally left Zack ✗ because she was miserable.
6. OK
7. Her new job was interesting ✗ and challenging.
8. OK
9. She picked up the phone ✗ and called Bill.

PRACTICE 2, page 147

Here are *both* ways each run-on sentence could have been corrected:

1. Bill answered the phone. It was Joanna calling.
   OR
   Bill answered the phone, and it was Joanna calling.
2. OK
3. Then he recognized her voice. He was surprised to hear from her.   OR
   Then he recognized her voice, but he was surprised to hear from her.

4. They talked on the phone for hours. Joanna told
   him about her divorce.   OR
   They talked on the phone for hours, and Joanna
   told him about her divorce.
5. OK
6. Bill was very happy to be with Joanna once more.
   Joanna fell in love with Bill all over again.   OR
   Bill was very happy to be with Joanna once more,
   and Joanna fell in love with Bill all over again.

PROOFREAD, page 147

Here is an example of how the corrected paragraph
should look. Yours may look slightly different.

Bill wasn't rich, but he had a decent job. Joanna
had her own job, **so** she didn't need a man to support
her. Joanna✗looked at Bill with new eyes. Bill was
talented, exciting, and adventurous. Joanna admired✗
and cherished him. They spent long hours on the
phone. **They** talked about all of their hopes✗and
dreams. Finally, Joanna✗and Bill got married. Her
new husband✗was not the perfect man. **He** left his
dirty clothes on the floor, and he often started arguments over little things. Joanna didn't mind too much✗
because Bill showed his love in many ways. **He** let
her live a happy life.

CHAPTER 9: MAKING
SENTENCES WORK TOGETHER
WRITE FOR THE MOMENT
PROOFREAD 1, page 150

Here is how the corrected paragraph should look:
VERB TENSE: present

Morris is a man of habit. Every weekend, he
does the same things. On Saturdays, he gets up early
and cleans the bathroom. Then he **goes** downstairs,
picks up the paper, and **puts** on the coffee. He drinks
his coffee and reads the paper for several hours. At
noon, he gets on the bus and **rides** to the supermarket.
There, he **buys** all the food he **needs** for the week.
Every Saturday night, he eats dinner in a restaurant
with a good friend, and then they **go** out to see a
show. On Sundays, Morris spends the morning at
church and then visits his elderly mother. They always **have** lunch together and **play** cards all afternoon. At the end of the day, Morris goes home and
eats supper. Every weekend is the same for Morris,
but he likes his routine.

PROOFREAD 2, page 150

Here is how the corrected paragraph should look:
VERB TENSE: past

Morris's mother had an interesting life when she
was a young woman. In 1920, she left her native
land and came to this country. She **learned** English
quickly and found a job in a clothing factory. She
was a talented singer and dancer, and soon she **found**
a job on the stage. She **started** out in the chorus,
but soon she **was** singing and dancing the lead. She
had a talent for comedy, and she **told** jokes between
the numbers. In her company, she met a young man
with as much talent as she. They **fell** in love and
got married. Soon they became a comedy team, and
they **traveled** around the country. They **were** very
popular in their time. After several years, they started
a family and decided to settle down in one place.
They both **got** regular jobs, but they **raised** their
children with a love of music and dance.

PROOFREAD 3, page 152

Here is how the corrected paragraph should look:

As a young man, Morris married the young
woman next door. Lilah **was** bright, talented, and
pretty. She played the piano and gave lessons. That
piano **drove** Morris crazy. It bothered him when he
was reading the paper or listening to the radio. In
addition, Lilah always wanted to know where he was
and what he was doing. Morris wanted out. Finally,
he **told** Lilah he **was** leaving. She **agreed** with his
decision right away. Lilah later became a famous
pianist, and she earned a lot of money. Nowadays,
Morris looks back on his past with a little regret.
After all, he is not rich or famous today. However,
he is basically happy with his bachelor life.

THE MYSTERIOUS *THEY*
PRACTICE, page 154

You may have thought of different words to fill in
the blanks. Have your instructor or a friend check
to be sure your words are appropriate for the sentence.

1. Pharmacists
2. Nurses
3. Dentists OR Orthodontists OR Oral surgeons
4. surgeon OR doctor OR cardiologist
5. medicine OR medication
6. room OR ward
7. flowers
8. father OR grandfather OR uncle OR brother OR
   son OR boss OR friend OR husband

PROOFREAD 1, page 155

Here is how the corrected paragraph should look:

Doctors serve us in different ways. They try to
cure and prevent disease. **People** go to doctors when
they are sick. They ask for help, understanding, and
advice.

Patients are sometimes unhappy with the treatment they receive. Sometimes they think that **the
doctor** is not good enough. Other times they feel
that he or she does not listen carefully or answer
important questions.

PROOFREAD 2, page 155

Here is how the corrected paragraph should look:

Drugs can be good or bad. They are good when they help **sick people** fight disease. They are bad when they are abused.

Drug abuse is a serious problem across the nation. It ruins lives. It even kills.

Many hospitals have special drug abuse treatment programs. **Some companies and schools** have drug counseling programs to help their workers or students. Fortunately, drug abuse is decreasing.

BACK TO THE SOURCE
PRACTICE 1, page 156

1. He
2. She
3. Mail carriers
4. A policeman
5. her
6. their
7. Counselors
8. themselves

PRACTICE 2, page 157

1. you
2. You
3. you
4. you
5. yourself

PROOFREAD, page 157

Here is how the corrected paragraph should look:

Counselors have difficult jobs. **They** must listen carefully to what **their** clients have to say. People who go to counselors are trusting them to be helpful and sympathetic. **They** must ask **themselves** if **they** are focusing completely on the clients' lives.

INDEX

a/an, 24
action verbs, 14, 43
adjectives, 79, 85
  comparative, 87–88
  superlative, 90–91
adverbs, 81, 84, 85
  comparative, 94
  irregular, 83
  superlative, 94
agreement
  pronoun-antecedent, 154, 156, 157
  subject-verb, 99, 107, 108, 109, 134
and
  in compound sentences, 122
  in compound verbs, 133, 134
  in series, 100
antecedents, 154, 156, 157
apostrophe
  in contractions, 40, 44
  in plural nouns, 71
  in possessive nouns, 70, 72

be/being, 14
  negatives with, 56
  past tense for, 45
  present tense for, 43
  questions with, 64
because, combining sentences with, 125
but, combining sentences with, 123

capital letter
  for I, 28
  to begin proper nouns, 22
  to begin sentences, 12
comma(s)
  in compound sentences, 122
  mistakes in using, 145, 146
  in series, 140, 141
  with transition words, 120, 142
common nouns, 22
comparative adjectives, 87–88
comparative adverb, 94
compound sentences, 122, 123, 124, 125
compound subjects, 100
  with pronouns, 101–2

compound verbs, 133, 134, 135
conjunctions, in compound sentences, 122, 123, 124, 125
contractions, 40, 44, 47, 56
cooperative adverbs, 94
count nouns, 67

double negatives, 59
double subjects, avoiding, 103

fragments, 115–19, 131
future tense, 40
  negatives in, 55

helping verbs, 46
here, 111–12

I, capital letter for, 28
indenting, first sentence in paragraph, 41
interrupting phrases, 104
irregular adverbs, 83
irregular comparatives, 88
irregular plural nouns, 27

main verbs, 46
more, comparatives with, 88, 89

negatives
  avoiding double, 59
  in present tense, 52
  with *be*, 56
  with future tense, 55
  with past tense, 54
noncount nouns, 67, 109
nouns, 21
  common, 22
  count, 67
  noncount, 67, 109
  plural, 25, 26, 27, 71, 72
  possessive, 70–72
  proper, 22

singular, 25
that are always plural, 108

object(s), 10, 18–19
object pronouns, 29, 30

paragraphs, 41, 149, 150
  fixing fragments in, 118–19
  indenting first sentence in, 41
  switchingtenses in, 151
  topic sentence in, 41
parallel structure, 143
past tense, 36, 37–38, 45
  continuous, 49
  negatives in, 54
  questions, 63
period, 12
phrases, interrupting, 104
plural nouns, 25, 26, 27, 71, 72
possessive nouns, 70
  plural, 72
possessive pronouns, 74–75
prepositions, 19
present tense, 33, 43
  continuous, 46–47, 57
  negatives in, 52
  questions, 61
pronouns
  antecedents for, 154, 156, 157
  compound subjects with, 101–2
  object, 29, 30
  possessive, 74–75
  reflexive, 76
  subject, 28, 30
  that are always singular, 107
proper nouns, 22

quantity expressions, 68–69
question mark, 12
questions, 10, 12
  with *be*, 64
  in continuous tense, 65
  past tense, 63
  present tense, 61
  subjects and verbs in, 17

reflexive pronouns, 76
run-ons, 127, 128, 131

sentence(s)
  complete, 10
  compound, 122, 123, 124, 125
  fragments in, 115–19, 131
  parallel structure in, 143
  parts of, 10
  run-ons, 127, 128, 131
  topic, 41
  types of, 10
series, commas in, 140, 141
so, combining sentences with, 124
spelling
  of adverbs, 82
  of comparative adjectives, 87–88
  of plural nouns, 26
  of verb forms, 34, 36, 47
statements, 10, 12
subject(s), 10, 16
  agreement with verb, 99, 107, 108, 109,
    134
  avoiding double, 103
  compound, 100, 101–2
  in questions, 17
subject pronouns, 28, 30
superlative adjectives, 90–91
superlative adverbs, 94

there, 111–12
topic sentence, 41
transition words, 120, 142

verb(s), 10
  action, 14, 43
  agreement with subject, 99, 107, 108,
    109, 134
  base form, 15
  being, 14, 43, 45, 56, 64
  compound, 133, 134, 135
  helping, 46
  main, 46
  in questions, 17
verb tense, 32
  future, 40, 55
  past, 36, 37-38, 45, 54
  past continuous, 49
  present, 33, 43, 52, 61
  present continuous, 46–47, 57
  present negatives, 52
  switching in paragraphs, 151